FURNITURE FUNDAMENTALS
Casework

POPULAR WOODWORKING BOOKS
CINCINNATI, OHIO
popularwoodworking.com

Contents

PROJECTS

Four Good Ways to Cut Rabbets

BY BILL HYLTON

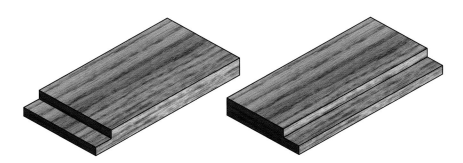

L-shaped cuts made with or across the grain are called rabbets – whether they are on the end or along the edge of the stock.

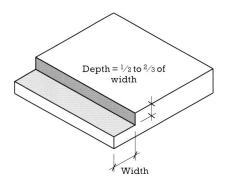

Depth = $1/2$ to $2/3$ of width

Width

The rabbet joint surely is one of the first ones tackled by new woodworkers. The rabbet is easy to cut, it helps locate the parts during assembly and it provides more of a mechanical connection than a butt joint.

I vaguely remember thinking, back when I was tackling my first home-improvement projects, that with practice I'd outgrow rabbet joints. Well I'm still cutting rabbets because woodworkers never outgrow them.

The most common form is what I call the single-rabbet joint. Only one of the mating parts is rabbeted. The cut is proportioned so its width matches the thickness of its mating board, yielding a flush fit.

The depth of the rabbet for this joint should be one-half to two-thirds its width. When assembled, the rabbet conceals the end grain of the mating board. The deeper the rabbet, the less end grain that will be exposed in the assembled joint.

In the double-rabbet joint, both the mating pieces are rabbeted. The rabbets don't have to be the same, but typically they are.

The rabbet works as a case joint and as an edge joint. Case joints generally involve end grain, while edge joints involve only long grain. In casework, you often see rabbets used where the top and/or bottom join the sides (end-grain to end-grain), and where the back joins the assembled case (both end-to-end and end-to-long). In drawers, it's often used to join the front and sides.

Because end grain glues poorly, rabbet joints that involve it usually are fastened,

Saw a rabbet on the table saw in two steps. Set the blade elevation and fence position first to cut the shoulder (above) then adjust either or both as necessary to cut the bottom.

either with brads, finish nails or screws concealed under plugs. (OK, in utilitarian constructions, we don't sweat the concealment.)

We don't necessarily think of the rabbet as an edge-to-edge joint, yet we all know of the shiplap joint. Rabbet the edges of the mating boards and nest them together. Voila!

It's also a great right-angle edge joint. We see this in the case-side-and-back combination, but also in practical box-section constructions such as hollow legs and pedestals. Long-grain joins long-grain in these structures. Because that glues well, you have a terrific and strong joint.

You can gussy up the joint's appearance by chamfering the edge of the rabbet before assembly. When the joint is assembled, the chamfer separates the face grain of one part from the edge grain of the other. Because the chamfer is at an angle to both faces, it won't look inappropriate even though its grain pattern is different.

One important variant is the rabbet-and-dado joint. This is a good rack-resistant joint that assembles easily because both boards are positively located. The dado or groove doesn't have to be big; often it's a single saw kerf, no deeper than one-third the board's thickness. Into it fits an offset tongue created

on the mating board by the rabbet.

The rabbet-and-dado joint is a good choice for plywood casework because it's often difficult to scale a dado or groove to the inexact thickness of plywood. It's far easier to customize the width of a rabbet. So you cut a stock-width dado, then cut the mating rabbet to a custom dimension. An extra cutting operation is required, but the benefit – a big one – is a tight joint.

There are lots of good ways to cut rabbets. The table saw, radial-arm saw, jointer and router all come to mind. The most versatile techniques use the table saw and router.

Rabbeting on the Table Saw

Rabbets can be cut at least two different ways on the table saw. Which method you choose may be influenced by the number of rabbets you have to cut, as well as the sizes and proportions of the workpieces.

It's quickest to cut the rabbets using whatever blade is in the saw. Two passes are all it takes. But if you have lots of rabbets to cut, or if the workpieces are too big to stand on edge safely, then use a dado cutter. (The latter is especially appropriate if your job entails dados as well as rabbets.) Let's look at the quick method first.

The first cut forms the shoulder. To set it up, adjust the blade height for the depth of the rabbet. There are a variety of setup tools you can use here, but it's always a good idea to make a test cut so you can measure the actual depth of the kerf.

That done, position the fence to locate the rabbet's shoulder. This establishes the rabbet width, so you measure from the face of the fence to the outside of the blade.

The cutting procedure is to lay the work flat on the saw's table, then run the edge along the fence and make the shoulder cut. If you are rabbeting the long edge of a board, use just the fence as the guide. When cutting a rabbet across the end of a piece, guide the work with your miter gauge and use the fence simply as a positioning device. It is easy to set up, and the miter gauge keeps the work from "walking" as it slides along the table saw's fence. Because no waste will be left between the blade and the fence, you can do this safely.

Nevertheless, if you feel uneasy about using the miter gauge and fence together, use a standoff block. Clamp a scrap (your standoff block) to the fence near the front edge of the saw's table. Lay the work in the miter gauge and slide it against the scrap. As you make the cut, the work is clear of the fence by the thickness of the scrap. (Try using a 1"-thick block to make setup easier.)

Having cut the shoulders of all the rabbets, you next adjust the setup to make the bottom cut. You may need to change the height of the blade or the fence position. You may need to do both.

Adjust the blade to match the width of the rabbet. Reposition the fence to cut the bottom of the rabbet, with the waste falling to the outside of the blade. Make that cut with the workpiece standing on edge, its kerfed face away from the fence.

When the workpieces are so large as to be cumbersome on edge – cabinet sides, for example – you want to cut the rabbets with a dado cutter. That way you can keep the work flat on the saw's table. Control the cut using a cutoff box or the fence. It's very easy to set the width of the cut with this approach.

Where the proportions of the workpiece allow it, use the rip fence to guide the cut. Clamp a sacrificial facing to the fence. Don't fret about the width of the stack, so long as it exceeds the width of the rabbet you want. Part of the cutter is buried in the fence facing, and you just set the fence to expose the width of the cutter that's working. Guide the work along the fence.

Alternatively, use a cutoff box to support the work and guide the cut. You get the same advantages in rabbeting that you do with dadoing: The work really doesn't move, the box does. Use a stop block to position the work to yield the width of rabbet you want. On the other hand, it may be a little more difficult to get exactly the cut width you want.

Rabbeting with the Router

The router is an excellent tool for rabbeting, in part because you can deploy it as a hand tool. For some jobs, you just want to immobilize the workpiece to your bench and move the cutting tool over it. In those situations, the router is the tool to use.

Occasionally, you might want to cut a rabbet into an assembly – perhaps a frame for a door or lid. If you use a router, you can wait until the frame is glued up and sanded, then produce the rabbet for a pane of glass or a panel. You do have to square the corners, but that's simple with a chisel.

Clamp a sacrificial facing – a strip of luan plywood here – to your table saw fence when cutting rabbets with a dado head. Run the cutter up into the facing, exposing only enough of the cutter to form the rabbet.

A major benefit of the hand-held router approach is that you can see the cut as it is formed. On the table saw (and the router table), the work itself conceals the cut.

You can cut rabbets on the router table as well, of course. But I want to focus on hand-held approaches here. Cutting a rabbet on the router table is quite similar to doing it on the table saw with a dado head.

A rabbeting bit is the commonly used cutter, but it is not the only one that will work. If you use an edge guide to control the cut, you can use a straight bit or a planer bit.

The rabbeting bit is piloted, and the typical bit makes a ⅜"-wide cut. Most manufacturers sell rabbeting sets, which bundle a stack of bearings with the cutter. Want to reduce the cut width? Switch to a larger bearing. The set I have yields six different widths from ½" to ⅛" (no ³⁄₁₆"), and with the largest bearing the bit can do flush trimming work.

The piloted bit enables you to rabbet curved edges. You can't do that on the table saw. Making a cut with a piloted rabbeting bit is pretty much a matter of setting the cut depth, switching on the router and diving in. Cut across the grain first, then with the grain. If you are routing only across the grain, either climb-cut in from the corner or clamp a backup scrap at the corner to prevent blowout as the bit exits the work.

The bit and the bearings do work very well, but I'm often inclined to use an unpiloted bit with an edge guide for rabbeting. I get an infinitely variable cut width with this setup, rather than a few predetermined widths. In addition, I have better control over the tool and the cut.

With a piloted bit alone, the cutting edges begin their work before the bearing makes contact with the edge. All too often, you dip around the corner of the workpiece at one end of the cut or the other. That doesn't happen with an edge-guide-controlled cut because the guide surface extends well beyond the cutter both fore and aft.

Keep the guide in contact with the workpiece edge throughout the feed – beginning before the cut actually starts and continuing until the bit is clear of the work – and you won't run into trouble.

The latter is especially true if you elect to circumvent blowout by climb-cutting in from a corner. The guide gives you the good control needed for a climb cut.

The edge guide is a big help in beginning and ending stopped or blind cuts as well. Brace the tip of the guide against the workpiece edge, shift the whole router as necessary to align the bit for the start of the cut, then pivot the router into the cut.

With an edge guide and straight bit, you can customize the rabbet's width, forming it in a series of passes.

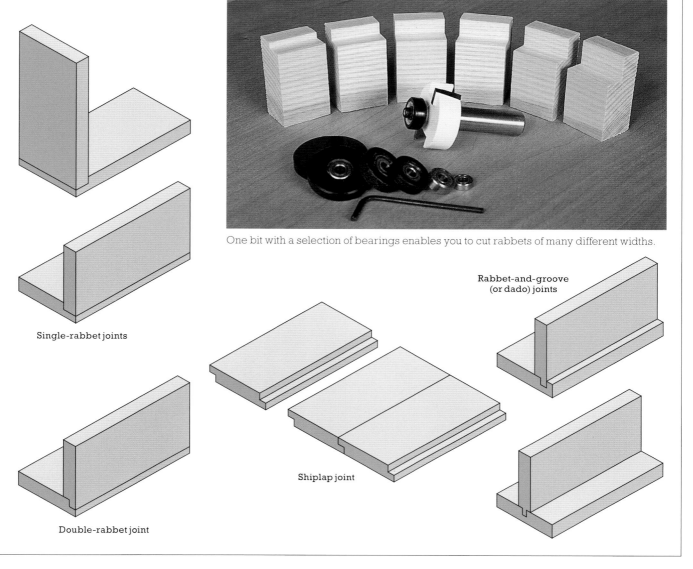

One bit with a selection of bearings enables you to cut rabbets of many different widths.

Single-rabbet joints

Double-rabbet joint

Shiplap joint

Rabbet-and-groove (or dado) joints

Dado Joints

BY BILL HYLTON

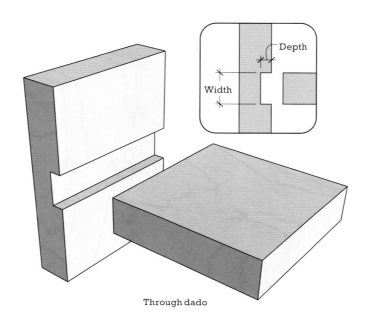

Through dado

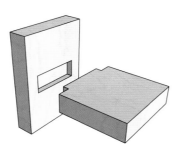

Blind dado

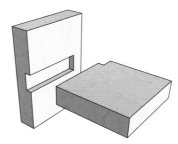

Stopped dado

In casework of any size, using natural or man-made materials (or both), the dado is prime-choice joinery. It follows that hoary adage of woodworking: "Use the simplest joint that will work."

It certainly works. The dado joint is traditional, with a centuries-long history of use in cabinetmaking.

It definitely is simple. All dado joint variations derive from the cut itself. A dado is a flat-bottomed channel cut across the grain of the wood. (When it runs with the grain, the channel is called a groove.) You cut a dado or groove into one board, and the mating board fits into it. One well-placed, properly sized cut with the proper tool makes the joint. And with today's power tools, it's a cut that is almost trivial to make – if you know how.

The dado does not have to be deep to create a strong joint. ⅛" is deep enough in solid wood, ¼" in plywood, medium-density fiberboard (MDF) or particleboard. The shallow channel helps align the parts during assembly, and the ledge it creates is enough to support the weight of a shelf and everything loaded on it. The dado also prevents the shelf from cupping.

The one stress it doesn't resist effectively is tension. In other words, it doesn't prevent the shelf from pulling out of the side. Only glue or fasteners can do that. Because all of the gluing surfaces involve end grain, the glue strength is limited.

Different Kinds of Dados

When the dado extends from edge to edge, it's called a through dado. It's easy to cut. The most common objection to it is that it shows. However, you can conceal the joint using a face frame or trim.

A dado or groove doesn't have to be through, of course. It can begin at one edge and end before it reaches the other (stopped), or it can begin and end shy of either edge (blind). This version is a little trickier to cut.

To make a stopped or blind dado, the corners of the mating board must be notched, creating a projection that fits in the dado. Sizing the notches so you have a little play from end-to-end makes it easier to align the edges of the parts. But it does sacrifice a bit of the strength that the narrow shoulder imparts.

A dado stack set consists of separate blades, chippers and washer-like shims. You fit the elements onto the saw's arbor, one by one.

Cutting Dados

There are some other joints that begin with dados, but before I even mention them, let's deal with the basic joinery cut. There are scads of ways to cut a dado successfully.

Keep a couple of criteria in mind as you tackle the dado cut. To end up with a strong joint, you need to make a cut of the correct width. The bottom needs to be smooth and flat, the sides perpendicular.

If the cut is too wide, glue isn't going to compensate; the joint will be weak. Get the fit right.

The two most obvious power tools for cutting dados are the table saw and the router. But there are other options.

You can do dados with a radial arm saw. If you are comfortable with this machine, you probably can recite the advantages. Fitted with a dado head, the radial arm saw hogs through dados

An accurate, shop-made cutoff box is the best guide accessory to use for dadoing on the table saw. Set the cutoff box on the sled base, tight against the fence. The work won't shimmy or shift out of position as you slide the box across the dado cutter.

quickly. The workpiece is face up, so you can see what you're doing. Layout marks are visible, and you can line up each cut quickly. When a stopped dado is needed, you can cut to a mark. The work isn't moved during the cut, so the piece is less likely to twist or shift out of position. This is especially helpful on angled cuts, whether a miter or a bevel (or both).

I have cut dados on narrow workpieces using a sliding compound miter saw. Most such saws have a cut-depth adjuster; you set the cut depth (with some trial and error), then "waste" each dado with kerf after kerf.

It's one of those operations you do once, just to try it. And once was enough for me. I prefer to stick with my table saw and my router for cutting dados.

Table Saw Dados

Let's look at the table saw first. It's powerful and equipped with accessories – a rip fence and a miter gauge – useful in positioning cuts. Like a lot of other woodworkers, I use a shop-made cutoff box (instead of the miter gauge) for crosscutting – it also works for dados. To use the saw effectively for dadoing, you need a dado cutter, either a stack set or a wobbler.

You can waste a narrow dado pretty quickly with whatever blade is on the saw. If you've got a manageable workpiece and just one or two dados to cut, you make five to seven kerfs to form each one. But to cut a cabinet's worth of dados, use a dado cutter.

If you're making cabinetry assembled with through-dado joints, you can knock out a lot of consistently sized and placed cuts in short order. What isn't necessarily quick and easy is achieving the precise width of cut you want. Stack sets, which give the cleanest cut, consist of separate blades and chippers. You have to select the combination needed to produce the approximate width of cut desired. To tune the cut to a precise width, you insert shims between the blades. It's got more trial-and-error in the setup than I like.

Some woodworkers (those with too much time on their hands, I think) make a chart or a cut sample with notes on the combinations of blades, chippers and specific shims needed to produce common-width dados. If you have the patience for this endeavor, my hat is off to you. Go for it.

But the woodworkers most likely to use the table saw for dadoing are those who are looking at a lot of cuts and not a lot of time to make them. Often, these folks adopt work-arounds to avoid protracted setups. They'll shoot for an undersized dado, and then plane or sand the part to be housed in it to fit. Or they'll use the dado-and-rabbet joint: The mating part is rabbeted to form a tongue that fits whatever dado has been cut.

How do you locate and guide the cut? The rip fence is seductive, because

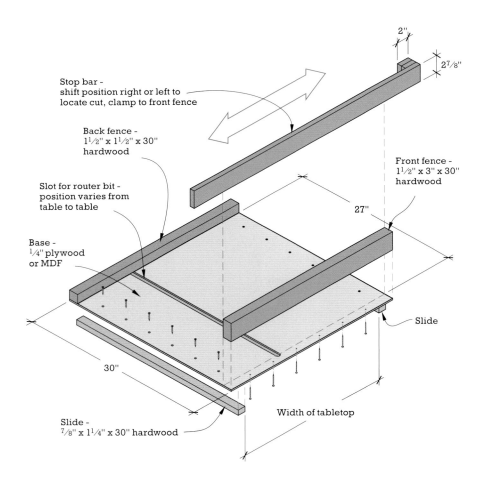

Stop bar -
shift position right or left to
locate cut, clamp to front fence

Back fence -
1¹/₂" x 1¹/₂" x 30"
hardwood

Slot for router bit -
position varies from
table to table

Base -
¹/₄" plywood
or MDF

Front fence -
1¹/₂" x 3" x 30"
hardwood

2"

2⁷/₈"

27"

Slide

30"

Slide -
⁷/₈" x 1¹/₄" x 30" hardwood

Width of tabletop

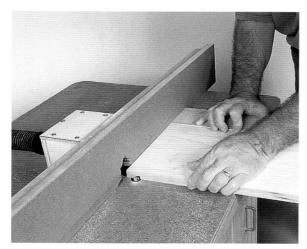

The typical router table setup works for dadoing parts like drawer sides. A push block – just a square scrap – stabilizes the work and backs up the cut, preventing tearout as the bit emerges from the cut.

Dado large workpieces on a router table with a cutoff-box-like sled. A stop clamped to the sled's fence locates the cut and immobilizes the work. Slides on the underside reference the edges of the tabletop to guide the sled.

it allows you to locate a cut consistently on both sides of a cabinet or bookcase. It eliminates the need for layout. But it isn't a crosscutting guide, and dados are crosscuts.

Of the two crosscutting guides, I prefer the cutoff box. It's built specifically for right-angle cuts and rides in both miter-gauge slots (instead of just one). In addition, it effectively immobilizes the workpiece, because the box is what moves, carrying the stationary workpiece with it. The work doesn't squirm or twist as you push it into the cutter. Fit the box with a stop so you can accurately and consistently locate a cut on multiples without individual layouts.

Stopped cuts can be problematic, and blind cuts can be downright hazardous. Because the work conceals the cutter, and because the cutoff box conceals most of the saw table, it's tricky to determine where to stop the cut. One good option is to clamp a stick to the outfeed table that stops your cutoff box at just the right spot.

A blind cut would require you to drop the work onto the spinning dado cutter. Not a routine that I'd recommend.

Any stopped cut done with a dado head will ramp from the bottom of the cut to the surface. You can leave it and simply enlarge the notch in the mating piece, but in so doing, you sacrifice the strength in the joint that comes from a tightly fitted shoulder. Better to chisel out the ramp.

Routing Dados

The router's often touted as the most versatile tool in the shop, and it certainly is useful for dadoing. The cutters offer convenient sizing: Want a ½"-wide dado? Use a ½" bit. Want a dado for ¾" plywood, which is typically under thickness? Use a $^{23}/_{32}$" bit. Changing bits is quick and easy.

The tool also offers options on approach. If you have your router hung in a table, dadoing with it is much like table saw dadoing. But the router gives you the option of moving the tool on a stationary workpiece, and in many situations, this turns out to be the better approach.

On the Router Table

For a long time, my mantra has been that you can rout grooves on a router table more easily than you can dados. Consider the typical router-table setup. It's small in comparison to the typical table saw setup, with its expansive infeed and outfeed tables. So I'd say, limit yourself to dadoing small parts only, things such as drawer sides.

Guided by the fence alone, you can easily rout grooves. The grain runs along a workpiece's long dimension, so a groove is easy to locate and cut guided by the fence.

But try guiding the workpiece's short dimension edge along the fence. Or locating a dado 16" from that edge.

Or 24" or 30". Maneuvering a 6'-long bookcase side or a 24" by 36" base cabinet side on a router table top is a joke. But a drawer side – where the piece is small and the dado (for the drawer back) is close to the end – can be routed pretty easily. You use a square-ended push block to keep the work square to the fence as you feed it and to back up the cut. Large case parts are best done on the table saw or with a hand-held router.

Recently, however, I made a cutoff box-like accessory for my big router table. I don't like miter gauges (or the slots they require) on a router table, so the dadoing box I made is guided by the tabletop's edges (see the drawing on page 10). I've dadoed some pretty large workpieces with it. The setup was simple, the operation downright easy and the results were clean and precise.

This accessory is changing my attitude, I must say. It offers all the advantages of the table saw-cutoff box setup, but eliminates the trial-and-error with the stack set.

You do need to use a stop to position the work, because the stop also prevents the bit from moving the work. The bit in a table-mounted router is spinning counterclockwise, and it will pull work to the right. You put the stop on the right to counteract that dynamic. (It's the equivalent of positioning the fence on the right.)

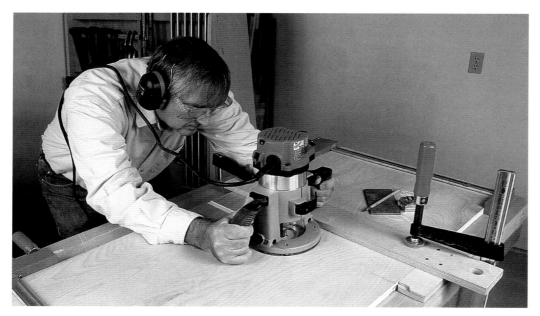

A crossbar attached at right angles to a plywood straightedge makes it an easy-to-align T-square guide for dadoing with a router. Clamp it securely to the work and the benchtop at each end.

The gap between the fence bases on my dadoing jig represents the cut width. Pinch scraps of the work material between them to set the jig.

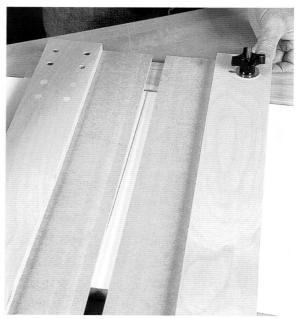

Position the jig by setting the fence base edge directly on your layout line. The crossbars ensure it will be perpendicular to the reference edge.

With a Hand-held Router

I'm not ready to entirely abandon the router as a hand-held tool, however. It remains a prime choice for dadoing large workpieces, such as sides for a tall bookcase or base cabinet. It seems easier and safer to move a relatively small tool on top of a cumbersome workpiece than the other way around.

The big question is how you will guide the router for the cut. A shop-made T-square fits the bill, as does a manufactured straight-edge clamp such as the Tru-Grip. An accurate T-square doesn't need to be "squared" on the work, as a Tru-Grip-type clamp does, but positioning it accurately can be a trick.

A setup gauge is helpful here. Cut a scrap to match the distance between the edge of the router baseplate and the near cutting edge of the bit. Align one edge of the gauge on the shoulder of the desired cut and locate the T-square (or other guide) against the opposite edge. Bingo. The guide is set.

Though more elaborate to construct, my favorite dadoing jig is easy to position on simple layout marks, and it adjusts easily to cut the exact width of dado you need. You size the jig to suit your needs.

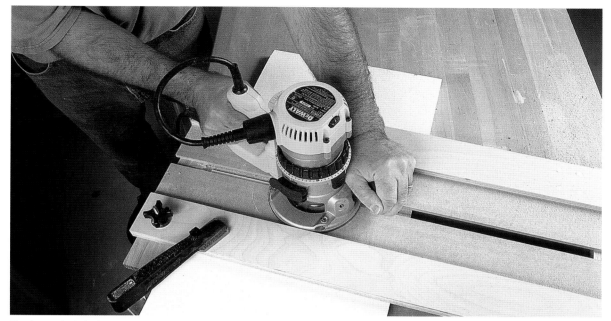

Cutting a dado is foolproof. The router is trapped between fences and can't veer off course, regardless of your feed direction. Reference the left fence as you push the router away, reference the right one as you pull it back, completing the cut.

The jig has two ½" plywood fences, each laminated to a ¼" plywood or MDF base strip. Both are matched to a particular router and bit by running that router along the fence, and trimming the thin base with the straight bit. One fence is then screwed to two hardwood crossbars.

The bars must be perpendicular to the fence, of course. The second fence is mounted so it can be adjusted toward or away from the fixed fence as shown in the photos.

Obviously, you cannot produce a dado narrower than the cutting diameter of the router bit, but you can do a wider one easily. Because the router is trapped between two fences, the feed direction is less of an issue and mis-cuts are unlikely.

The bases make it easy to adjust the cut width and to position the jig on simple layout marks. To do the former, use a scrap or two of the stock to be housed in the cut as gauges. Set them against the fixed-fence base, slide the adjustable fence into position and lock it down. To do the latter, align the fixed-fence directly on one of the marks, with a crossbar tight against the work's edge. Secure the jig to the work with two clamps.

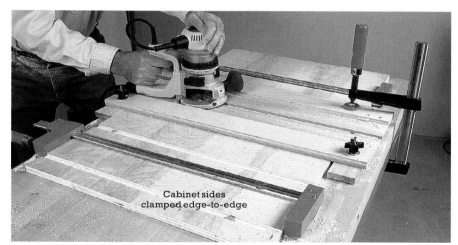

Dadoing cabinet sides? Clamp them edge-to-edge and rout both at the same time for cuts that line up perfectly.

For stopped or blind dados, clamp stop blocks to the jig (rather than the work). Move the jig, and the stops move with it. Using the plunge base eases beginning and ending these cuts.

JOINERY

Biscuits: Fast, Cheap & Good

BY BILL HYLTON

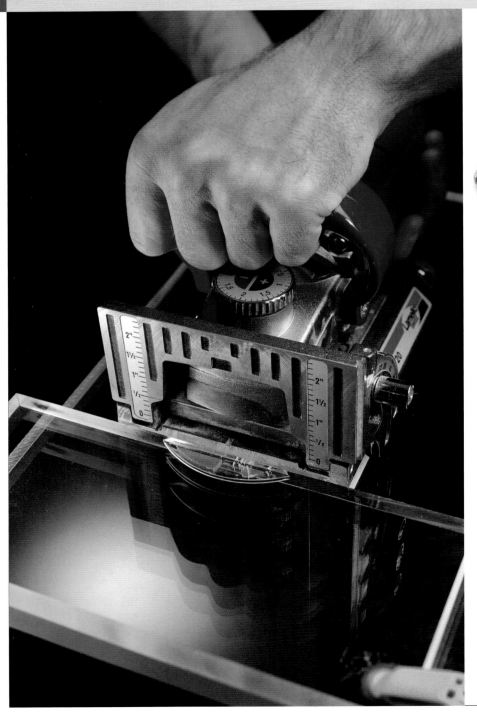

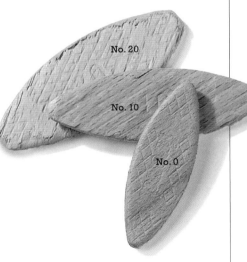

Biscuit joiners cut a slot the perfect size for a biscuit. To illustrate how one works, we cut some Lexan, a tough polycarbonate plastic. Though this isn't a common application for the tool, it handled the job with ease.

Biscuit joinery is so fast and easy it almost seems like cheating. And I gotta tell you, I'm no cheater. Consequently, I pretty much ignored the system, sticking with more traditional joinery, even when I was working with plywood and other sheet goods.

Then about three years ago, while working on a book about chests with drawers, I crossed paths with Mark Edmundson who exposed me to a novel (to me, anyway) method of post-and-panel construction. The posts and rails of a chest he designed and built were joined with loose tenons, while the maple-veneered medium-density fiberboard panels were joined to the posts and rails with biscuits.

Don't misjudge Edmundson. He's a graduate of James Krenov's demanding course at the College of the Redwoods. He's capable of hand-cut joints. But when a client has a limited budget, the best way to reduce costs is to design something that goes together quickly. Hence, he sometimes uses sheet goods and biscuit joinery in his work. Speed and economy are the whole point of biscuit joinery.

Biscuitry Basics

For the uninitiated, a biscuit joint is a butt joint splined with a small beech wafer – the biscuit. Simple in appearance, biscuits are fairly sophisticated. Shaped like tiny, flattened footballs, they're stamped out, a process that (in most cases) compresses them. Add moisture and they swell up.

The linchpin of the process is a dedicated portable power tool known as a biscuit joiner. The tool enables you to plunge a cutter into a workpiece to make a slot that will, unsurprisingly, accommodate half a biscuit.

To make a simple biscuit joint, you cut a slot into each mating surface, insert a biscuit into one slot, then slide the mating part into position. As you close the joint, the protruding biscuit half penetrates the second slot.

Here's where the reason that biscuits are compressed becomes clear. When you use ordinary yellow glue, the moisture in the glue prompts the biscuit to swell. The biscuit then locks in the matching slots and strengthens the joint. When you use polyurethane glue or an

For a case, large or small, align the sides and clamp a straightedge to them – I'm using a shelf here – to position the biscuit joiner. A few quick plunge cuts and the joint is ready for assembly.

With the shelf butted against the bench vise's dog (or some other stop), you can cut biscuit slots with both hands on the tool. No layout here, because the edge of the tool's base is aligned with the edge of the work-piece.

epoxy, you should dampen a biscuit with water as you insert it in its slot so it can expand and lock.

The result is a joint that's pretty easy to produce, invisible and surprisingly strong.

Biscuits can be used to reinforce – to spline, in effect – almost any butted joint: edge-to-edge, edge-to-face, end-to-edge, end-to-face, case miters or frame miters. The qualification is that the contact surface between the mating parts must be thick enough and wide enough to accommodate one of the three common biscuits – No. 0 (the smallest), No. 10 or No. 20 (the largest).

In the more common biscuit joints, you will use more than one, arraying them in a line across a wide piece or, for thicker stock, stacking them.

Biscuits are most appropriate when used in casework produced using sheet goods – plywood, melamine, veneered MDF, etc. Often, these sheet goods are selected for a project to circumvent lumber preparation and panel glue-ups; in other words, you're trying to shorten the production time. So a joinery application that also shortens production time – without sacrificing strength or accuracy – is appropriate.

When stock thickness is more than 1", you should stack at least two biscuits evenly.

Cutting the Slots

Many of the benefits of biscuit joinery derive from the tool itself. The biscuit joiner has only one purpose – cutting slots for biscuits – so it's always set up for the operation.

Once in a while you may need to adjust the machine for a different biscuit size, but this involves nothing more than a twist of a small knob to change the depth of the cutter's plunge into the work.

The tool has two reference surfaces: the base and the fence. Every joiner is designed to locate the center of the slot ⅜" from the base, centering the slot on the ¾" edge of the stock. The front of the joiner will have a registration mark indicating the vertical centerline of the slot.

Fence designs vary, with some being easier and more precise to adjust. You should be able to adjust the angle of the fence and its elevation above the blade. Bear in mind that not all fences are aligned perfectly with the cutter, and not all stay locked.

Rule No. 1 is to always use the same reference surface for slotting both parts of any joint. On the tool, your first choice should be the base, simply because the machine's design virtually guarantees it to be accurate. It's easy to hold the tool steady when it's resting squarely on its base, but much more difficult when it's hanging from the fence.

(Keep in mind that the nose of the tool must be square to the surface being slotted. If the slot isn't cut square to the surface, the joint won't line up.)

If the location of the slot needs to be shifted, use a shim under either the tool or the work. You'll find, as I have, that you can orient the work and the tool so you can use the base as a reference to produce slots for any form of biscuit joint.

On the workpieces, the reference surfaces should be those that must line up in the final assembly. For example, say you need the top surface of a case top to be flush with the top edge of the case side and you want to use the biscuit joiner's base as the reference. Just slot the top with its top surface facing down and slot the side with the joiner's base flush against the side's top edge. One good way to accomplish the latter is to butt the side's end against a "fence" held in a bench vise. Stand the joiner on its nose with the base against the fence and make the cut.

To accomplish that with case miters, just clamp the mating elements face-to-face so the bevels form a "V," then set the joiner into the "V." The tool will rest on one bevel while slotting the mate.

Laying it All Out

Layout is simple – place the parts together the way you want them to be in the assembled joint, mark the center of each slot on the mating pieces and align the joiner's registration mark to cut the slot.

Typically, that's all the layout necessary. Occasionally, you'll have to extend the mark across an edge or onto a face so it's visible when the joiner is in position to cut the slot. You don't need to address the slot's vertical position because that's determined by the tool's fence or base.

In a wide joint – where you'll join a bottom to a side in a 2'-deep cabinet, for example – you'll need to use several biscuits. The generally recognized rule of thumb is to space biscuits 6"-8" apart on center. Offset the biscuits on the ends about 3" from the edge of the workpiece.

Stacking your slots is common when the thickness of the working stock exceeds 1". If your material is all the same thickness, you can cut a slot, then roll the piece over and cut the second. When a piece is thicker or thinner than its mates, the best approach is to use a shim under the joiner's base to elevate it when cutting the second slot.

Assembly

When putting the biscuit joint together, it's essential to get enough glue in the mating slots and on the biscuit to promote expansion. But be discrete – you don't want glue welling out of the slots.

You can buy applicators designed especially for biscuit slots. I usually run the glue-bottle's tip along the edge of the slot, then use an artist's brush to spread it through the slot. I run a bead from slot to slot, and I use the brush to spread it, too. When the glue is applied to both parts, I stuff a biscuit in each slot, seat it firmly and move on.

Be wary of gluing biscuits in one at a time, and of trying to apply glue to all the joints in an assembly before closing any of them. The biscuits can swell before

Make sure glue gets into the biscuit slot, because it's the moisture that causes the biscuit to swell and produce a strong joint. I use an old artist's brush to work glue through the slots.

you want them to and make assembly difficult.

A benefit of biscuit joinery is that your case will clamp up square if your parts are squarely cut. The scramble to wrench the case into proper alignment before the glue sets up is reduced to a low-key measuring of diagonals to confirm what you already know.

Working Routine

A small wall cabinet I made recently is a good example of how I used biscuit joinery. I set two shelves, a top and a bottom between the sides using biscuit joints. I then assembled a face frame of very narrow members, again using biscuit joints. I glued the frame to the case, and used five biscuits to help locate it.

Because of the narrowness of the sides (they are less than 10"), I used only two biscuits per joint, and I placed them by aligning the joiner base's edge with the edge of the side or the shelf. The only layout needed was to mark where the shelves crossed the sides.

The shelves were laid flat on the benchtop for slotting. A straightedge clamped across the two sides served as a fence when I slotted the sides with the joiner on its nose, its base against the fence.

In making the face frame, I used half a biscuit to join the top rail to the stiles. To do this, I used the rail's top edge as my centerline in slotting the ends, and in marking the stiles for slotting. The assembled frame had biscuits jutting out the top; these I sawed off (and with the cabinet hung on the wall, you don't see that).

Finally, the locations of the biscuits between the frame and the case were marked with the frame carefully aligned – without using any glue, of course – on the case and clamped. I stood the case and the face frame on end to slot them for the biscuit at the top, then set them both on their side to slot them for the side biscuits.

The completed cabinet isn't fine furniture, but it went together quickly, it looks good and it's solid. Using the biscuits isn't cheating – it's just working smart.

Face frame members often are too narrow for a full biscuit. The biscuit that joins this stile to the top rail will have to be trimmed after assembly. Because the frame's top edge will be concealed in the completed cabinet, the open joint won't be a problem.

The primary value of biscuit joints between face frames and casework is alignment. Only a few biscuits are needed to ensure that.

The Case for Case Miters

BY BILL HYLTON

Try this with a garden-variety case miter joint. The lock miter joints hold your parts together on their own, freeing both your hands to apply clamps.

What joint would you use at the corners of a case? If appearance is a consideration – when is it not? – you definitely don't want an ugly joint like a rabbet. No matter how thin, that strip of exposed end grain – the butt of the board – is unattractive.

From the standpoint of what looks best, the miter joint should be atop your list. The only surfaces visible are the attractive ones: the faces and the edges. If you are making a small chest and you have a wide, long board with killer figure, you can wrap that figure around the corners without interruption.

You may think of the case miter as being difficult in subtle ways. Well, yes, it can be. If the joinery cuts are off by a degree or two, the joint isn't going to be square no matter what you do. Gluing and clamping the parts can be an exercise in torment and despair. There's no mechanical interlock to hold the parts in alignment, and glue just enhances the natural tendency of the surfaces to creep.

Moreover, despite the fact that a miter joint has more gluing surface than a butt joint, the glued miter joint isn't that strong. The shortcoming is that the miter brings end grain to the glue-up session.

But simple solutions to these and other difficulties do exist, and the results make it a joint worth mastering.

Case Miter Varieties

Let's look first at some of the ways the joint can be shaped to reinforce it, and to make assembly and clamping easier and more effective. The most basic miter joint is made by beveling the mating edges of both parts at 45°, then butting these edges together.

Surely the easiest way to make the joint simpler to align is by using biscuits. If you have a biscuit joiner, you know it takes only a minute to set the fence and cut slots in both parts. The biscuits make alignment easy and they offer some reinforcement to the joint as well.

Another joint worth learning to master is a routed lock miter joint because it gives the appearance of a miter but introduces an interlock, expands the glue area and makes assembly and clamping foolproof. We'll come back to that in a little while.

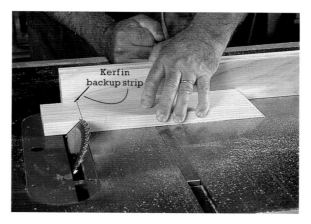

A backup strip attached to the miter gauge aids when you are trying to locate the bevel cut. Align your layout line with the kerf in the strip.

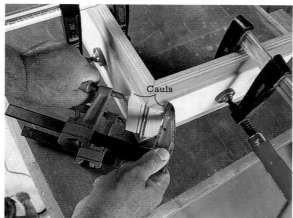

A sure way to assemble case miters is with shop-made miter-clamping cauls. Clamp a caul to each half of the joint, then apply clamps. Do one joint at a time.

Sawing the Bevels

Accurate 45° bevels on the mating parts are essential for the case miter. You could cut the bevels using a radial-arm saw, compound-miter saw or sliding compound-miter saw. But the capacity of the latter two saws is limited, typically less than 12", and all three saws can have some accuracy shortcomings.

You'll most likely want to cut the bevels on a table saw. Tilt the blade to 45° and, depending on the proportions of your workpiece, guide the work through the saw with the miter gauge or along the rip fence. It's pretty cut and dry, until you run into one (or more) of the problems that often come up.

First of all, be wary of kickback. If you're using the rip fence, you always want the saw blade to tilt away from it. With the blade tilted toward the fence, the offcut is trapped between the blade and the fence, and it's all but certain to fire back toward you.

If you have a left-tilt saw, the customary fence location (to the right of the blade) is the safe one for bevels. But most

saws are right-tilters, and with those saws the fence will have to be moved to the left of the blade. In any event, be sure you stand to the left of the blade, clear of "Kickback Alley."

The most disheartening problem is the one that isn't evident until all the joints are cut and you start assembling them. This is when you discover that the bevel angle is off a degree or two, and the joints aren't square. Maybe you didn't tilt the blade enough, but more likely the fault is hiding in the adjustment and alignment of the saw.

You should know if you can trust the scale on your saw when you tilt the blade for this cut. If you aren't absolutely certain it is accurate, use a drafting triangle to check the blade's angle. Crank the blade to its maximum height, tilt it, then check it. Make sure the triangle is flat against the saw blade's body and not against a carbide tip.

Double-check the angle by making a pair of test cuts and join the two samples. If the corner they form is square, your setup is right and you can proceed.

You won't always use the rip fence. If the edge being beveled is the short one, you'll want to use the miter gauge. This common accessory is, of course, another source of inaccuracies. If you use your miter gauge, make sure you square it to the blade with a drafting triangle before tilting the blade.

Instead of a miter gauge, a lot of us use a crosscut sled to ensure we get square cuts. The sled can be used for bevels, too.

If you make a lot of bevel cuts and think it's worth the materials and shop time, you can make a sled exclusively for bevel cuts. If you do this, you'll derive a couple of benefits. One is the unmistakable angled kerf you can use to align the workpiece. Another is the zero-clearance around the kerf, which helps minimize chipping on the underside of the workpiece. If you work with veneered or melamine-coated sheets, this is a benefit you'll really appreciate.

Finally, if you are using a contractor's saw, you may be reluctant to tilt the blade at all. Doing that can throw some saws out of alignment. Instead of tilting the blade, you can use an angle sled to deliver the work to the blade. In this case, the workpiece is tilted instead of the blade.

Aligning the work for the cut is less straightforward than you might think. If you're using the crosscut sled or a miter gauge with a backup strip, you have a kerf to use.

But there's no practical way to measure directly from the tilted blade to position the fence. Instead, you have to lay out the bevel cut on the stock and align the layout line with the blade. Then bring the fence into position. It's easy to do this with your stock on the outfeed side of the blade.

Assembly

The biggest problem you will confront when assembling a case miter is applying clamp pressure without forcing the joints out of alignment. V-blocks, lined with packing tape to shed glue, can hold the tips of the bevels together, but other strategies work, too.

Glue tack often holds a small box together while you position pressure blocks and apply clamps. Or you can use packing tape to hold the parts while you apply the clamps. Tape the outside of the joint before adding glue.

With a chest or cabinet, the parts are larger, more cumbersome and less cooperative. In this situation, it may be practical to address one joint at a time. Glue up two joints individually, then wait for the glue to set before combining them into the box or case.

Also, adding biscuits or splines to the joint makes it easier to align and hold the pieces in place while you position the blocks and apply the clamps.

Lock Miter Joint

The routed lock miter sets off in a very different construction direction. You get that attractive miter-joint appearance, but you use a table-mounted router and a "trick" bit to cut it. When the time comes for assembly, the joint aligns perfectly and you can apply clamps without pressure blocks.

The bit's trick is that one setup suffices for cuts on both pieces you want joined. When you have the bit adjusted spot-on and the fence perfectly positioned, you're golden. Just lay one panel flat on the tabletop and slide it along the fence to rout it. Stand the mating panel upright against the fence to make the mating cut on it.

There are two parts to the setup process: setting the bit height and then setting the fence position. You have to make gross settings of both before cutting anything. Then, through a series of test cuts, you hone in on the optimum settings, first of the bit height, then of the fence position. Here's how:

Positioning a Rip Fence for Bevel Cuts

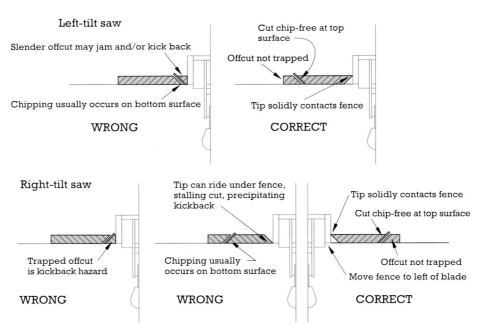

Half of each lock miter joint is cut with the work flat on the top of the router table. Using a push block helps you hold the workpiece down while you advance it across the bit.

Stand the work on end flat against the fence to rout the other half of the joint. A featherboard keeps the workpiece against the fence, obviating the need for a tall fence facing.

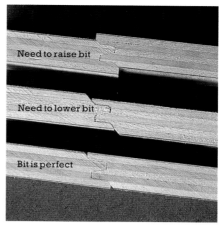

Adjust the lock miter bit up or down based on your test cuts. Halve the sample and fit the resulting two pieces together to see how they fit.

• *Setting the Bit Height:* The key is lining up the midpoint of the bit with the center of the stock. The midpoint of the bit is on the very slightly angled edge of the interlock, as shown in the illustration below.

The best thing you can do is mark the centerline on a scrap piece of the working stock, set it beside the bit, hunker down and squint across the tabletop to line them up. Maybe you'll nail the alignment, but it'll probably take a test cut and an adjustment (or two) to get it just right.

Having set an approximate bit height, move the fence into position to guide your first test cut. I stand a piece of the working stock "behind" the bit and sight along the fence to the bit. My objective is to have the stock aligned with the profile's bottom edge.

Make a test cut with the sample flat on the table. Cut it in half, turn one of the pieces over and join the two. If the faces are flush, the bit setting is perfect. If they are offset, an adjustment is needed, as shown below.

Use the depth-bar of a dial caliper to measure the offset between the two test pieces. Raise or lower the bit half the measurement. (Having a good depth-adjustment system on your router and table is a boon here.)

• *Setting the Fence:* When cutting the joint, you're dealing with a 45° bevel. The exposure of the cutting edge above the table and in front of the fence must match the thickness of the working stock. Because the bit is set, it's no longer a variable. Only the fence position is in play. If the fence is set too far back, a cut will remove too much stock and alter the length or width of the workpiece. If it is too far forward, you won't get the full miter. You already have a gross setting; now you just need to refine it.

To set your fence correctly, cut a scrap piece from the working stock, feeding only a few inches into the cut.

• If the tip is square, move the fence back to expose more of the bit.

• If the cut is shortening the material, pull the fence forward so that it will be able to house more of the bit.

• If the tip comes to an acute angle whose tip is flush with the square, unrouted edge of the stock, the fence position is just right.

With the final fence position set, you can proceed to the real workpieces.

Setting Up a Lock Miter Bit

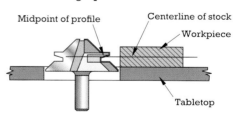

1. Set bit height, aligning midpoint of the profile with the centerline of stock

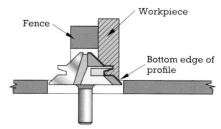

2. Set the fence back from the bottom of the profile by the thickness of the working stock

Box Joints

BY BILL HYLTON

Visit most any antiques store or flea market, and you're sure to see stacks of old wooden boxes marked with the logos of by-gone businesses. Small boxes for cigars, big ones for fruit and lots of in-between sizes. All are assembled at the corners with interlocking square pins or fingers – the box joint.

The box joint is a sort of square-cut through dovetail. It's used in the same situations as the dovetail – assembling boxes, drawers and casework. It has pretty fair mechanical strength, but what it does is create a tremendous amount of gluing surface to create a stout joint.

You may know this joint as a finger joint. I use that name for an interlocking edge-to-edge joint that's cut with a special bit.

Look at the box-jointed object at left. The end of the piece on top is comb-like, with uniform pins and slots. The pins on this board fit into the slots on its mate and vice versa. So making the joint is all about cutting a series of slots to form a series of pins.

You can cut the slots in several ways. The most obvious is on the table saw with a dado cutter. Make a little jig to attach to the miter gauge – or an independent one that rides in both miter slots – and go to town. But the table-mounted router does a clean job, too, and in the same amount of time.

The Box-joint Jig

Whether you do the work on the table saw or the router table, the process is the same, and so is the jig. What the jig does is position the work so the cuts are separated by pins that are the same size as the cuts. The critical element is a little wooden "key." The key is custom-made, so it fits the cut exactly. It's attached to the jig in a way that permits lateral adjustment so you can control the spacing of the cuts.

The box-joint jigs I've made are miter-gauge-like, with a separate facing into which the key is glued. The jig itself can be any scrappy old thing, so long as it's accurate, with the back perpendicular to the saw or router table. You can change the facing as dictated by wear and use.

While you probably can get acceptable results cutting ½"-deep slots on a jig set up for a ¾" depth-of-cut, splintering

or "blow-out" is likely to occur as the bit exits a cut. The backing is ¼" above where the tip of the blade or bit cuts through the workpiece, which is as good as no backing at all.

While it's possible to reuse a facing, it may be better to use a fresh pair of slots – not necessarily a fresh facing – for each new job. (By sliding the facing fully right for one job, then fully left for another, and then rotating it 180° and repeating, you should be able to use a single facing for at least four jobs. Then you can trim it down and drill new mounting holes and use it for a couple more.)

I made an independent box-joint jig for the table saw (shown on page 24) that rides in both miter slots and has the capacity for blanket-chest-size parts. Candidly, I haven't used it on anything bigger than roughly 2'-square, 8"-high drawers. The particulars are shown in the illustration above.

To make the jig, select suitable materials from your scrap pile. I used sheet goods (plywood and MDF, primarily) for most parts because they're stable, and because I always seem to have odd scraps around. The "key" is the one part of the jig that should always be a hard wood. It's subjected to a lot of wear, and

if it's too soft, it will deform and throw off the accuracy of your cuts. The pins won't mesh, in other words. Except for the replaceable facing, glue and screw the parts together.

My router tables are devoid of miter-gauge slots. So for router-table use, I have a small box-joint sled, also shown on page 24. To guide it, I clamp hardboard or plywood strips to the tabletop – the sled is then trapped between them. These fences allow the workpieces to extend beyond the jig's edge. You can cut joints on wide stock as easily as on narrow boards.

Using the Jig

The initial step is to reconcile the slot width and the width of the workpieces. You really want to begin and end each array of pins with a full pin or a full slot. To accomplish this, the width of the boards should be evenly divisible by the slot width. If this isn't the case, then it's best to change either the slot width or the joint width.

A corollary is that a joint layout that begins with a full pin and ends with a full slot mates two identical pieces. Therefore you can cut both at the same time. All four parts of a box can even be cut simultaneously.

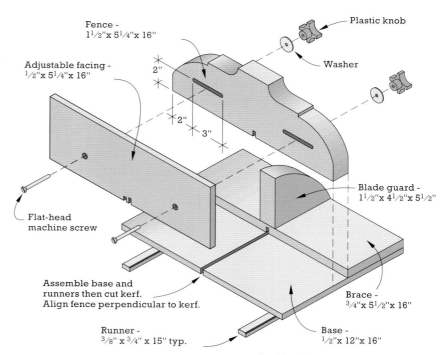

Fence -
1½"x 5¼"x 16"

Adjustable facing -
½"x 5¼"x 16"

2"

2"

3"

Plastic knob

Washer

Blade guard -
1½"x 4½"x 5½"

Flat-head
machine screw

Assemble base and
runners then cut kerf.
Align fence perpendicular to kerf.

Runner -
⅜" x ¾" x 15" typ.

Brace -
¾"x 5½"x 16"

Base -
½"x 12"x 16"

Position the base on the slides so that
the blade is centered on the base.

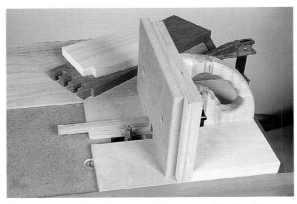

The jig I use on the table saw rides in both miter-gauge slots. The adjustable facing, into which the key is glued, is cut from a scrap of $1/2$" MDF.

On the router table, I use a small version of the jig. My tables don't have miter-gauge slots, so I align the jig with the selected bit in the slot in the jig base. Then I set a thin plywood strip against either edge of the jig and clamp them to the tabletop.

If the layout begins and ends with a full pin, you must cut the sides and ends in sequence. I'll explain this in just a few more paragraphs.

It's worth pointing out that the stock thickness has no bearing on the pin thickness. You can use $1/4$" pins on $3/4$" stock, for example, or $1/2$" pins on $3/8$" stock. But it does impact the pin length. The blade or bit elevation must equal the stock thickness (plus the jig base thickness, of course).

Set up the cutter and jig. Install the dado cutter in the table saw, combining the blades and chippers needed for the desired cut width. In a table-mounted router, use the correct diameter of straight bit. Adjust the height. The easiest way to set this is to lay a scrap of the working stock on the jig base, park it by the cutter and raise the cutter to that height.

The first cut creates a slot in the facing for the key. What I do is offset the facing to the left to begin. Lock the facing and cut a slot, as shown on the top of page 25.

The next step is to make a key that just fits the slot. The key must be the exact width of the slot, but no taller. So your key is on the order of $1/2$" wide and $3/8$" thick, maybe smaller, maybe larger. I rip a stick close, then hand plane it (it's occasionally unavoidable) to fit. When it fits, I clip it in two and glue one piece into the slot.

To adjust the jig for the joinery cuts, set the second piece of the key against the cutter and slide the facing toward it until its key touches the loose one. The gap between the cutter and the key now equals the bit's diameter.

Cut a test joint. Stand a stacked pair of samples in the jig, edges snug against the key. Cut a slot. Move the stack, fitting the slot over the key. Cut another slot. Repeat the process until all the pins are formed.

Fit the joint together (offset them if need be to align pins with slots). If the pins won't go into the slots, the key is too far from the cutter. If the pins are loose in the slots, the key is too close to the cutter.

Rather than slide the facing left or right a "hair," a "tad" or a "skoshe," use your dial calipers. Measure a pin and a slot. The amount you move the facing is half the difference between the pin width and the slot width. You can use a feeler gauge to make what is most likely a minute adjustment.

• If the pin is bigger than the slot, move the key closer to the cutter. Set a block against the key and clamp it. Loosen the facing, slip the feeler gauge between the block and the key, and w the facing. Remove the block.

• If the slot is bigger than the pin, move the key away from the cutter. Clamp the block to the jig with the feeler gauge between it and the key. Loosen the facing, remove the gauge, and reset the facing with the key tight against the block. Then remove the block.

A second set of cuts will confirm the accuracy of your adjustment.

One note about fitting the joints: If your joint is long, with a dozen or more pins, you must be wary of cumulative error. A discrepancy of $1/128$" doesn't have a significant impact when the joint has six pins. But double or triple that number and you may have a joint that won't close. So the bigger the joint, the more exacting your setup must be.

Cutting the Joints

There's no reason to cut the parts one at a time. It's tedious work, so you'll appreciate anything you can do to expedite it.

As I already mentioned, if your joint layout begins with a pin and ends with a slot, you can cut sides and ends simultaneously, four parts in a stack.

As with the test cut, you align the parts in the stack, stand them on the jig base, upright against the back. Butt the edges against the key. Cut. Step the stack over the key and cut. Step again and cut again. Repeat and repeat until the last slot is cut.

If one piece begins and ends with pins, the mate will begin and end with slots, as shown on page 25. They must be cut in sequence. You can, of course, pair up parts of a box, but you can't cut all four parts at once.

Start with the piece that begins and ends with pins. Cut the slots in it. After the last slot has been cut, step that slot over the key. Stand the mating piece beside it, edge to edge, as shown. Cut. Remove the first piece and slide its mate to the right, the slot over the key. Cut again. Step and cut until all the slots are completed.

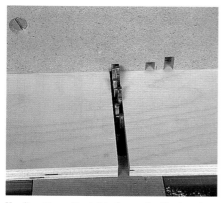

Kerfing the adjustable fence for the key is the first step in setting up your box-joint jig. Note the two kerfs from a previous job to the right of the blade. It's best, I think, to set up fresh for each new job.

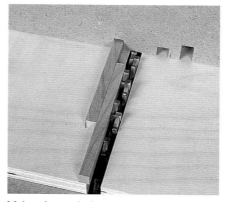

Make a key strip, hand-planing it to achieve a tight press-fit in the kerf. Cut the strip into two pieces: one is the key, the second is a setup gauge.

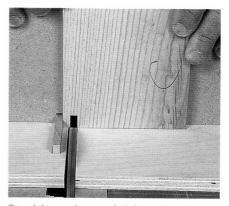

Stand the work on end, tight against the key. Push the jig across the cutter and make the first slot.

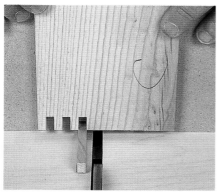

After each cut, step the work to the right, fitting the freshly cut slot over the key. Each cut matches the width of the key, and leaves a pin of the same thickness between slots. Step-and-repeat until you've cut pins across the full width of the work.

Cutting the full layout across both pieces isn't necessary to test the fit. If the setup is significantly off, fitting three or four pins will expose it. If those pins mesh nicely, cut more of them and refit the joint.

In production mode, you can cut more than one board at a time. Stack the sides and cut the pins across an end. Then hold the ends against the sides to continue the cutting sequence across them.

If the joint layout begins with a pin and ends with a slot, then all four parts are identical, and all can be cut at the same time.

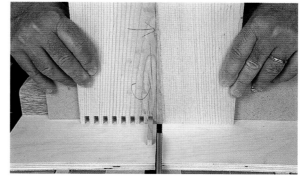

If the layout on a board begins and ends with a pin, the mating piece must begin and end with a slot. To align the work for the beginning slot, butt the piece against its mate.

Mortise & Tenon Basics

BY CHRISTOPHER SCHWARZ

A lot of woodworkers spend a lot of time, effort and money to avoid making mortise-and-tenon joints. Biscuits, dowels, commercial loose-tenon jigs and expensive router bits are just a few of the "work-arounds" developed this century so you don't have to learn to make a mortise and its perfectly matched tenon.

But once you learn how straightforward and simple this joint can be, you will use it in every project. Why? Well, it is remarkably strong. A few years ago we decided to pit this venerable and traditional joint against the high-tech super-simple biscuit. So we built two cubes, one using biscuits and one with mortises and tenons. Then we dropped a 50-pound anvil on each cube. The results were eye-opening.

Both cubes were destroyed. The biscuit cube exploded on impact. Some of the biscuits held on tightly to the wood, but they pulled away chunks from the mating piece as the joint failed.

The second cube survived the first hit with the anvil – the joints held together even though the wood split at the points of impact. A second hit with the anvil ruined the cube entirely, though most of the tenons stuck tenaciously to their mortises.

The lesson here is that biscuits are indeed tough, but when they fail, they fail catastrophically. The mortise-and-tenon joints fail, too, but they take their time, becoming loose at first rather than an immediate pile of splinters.

So when you're building for future generations and you know how to make this stout joint with minimal fuss, you won't say "Why bother?" You'll say "Why not?"

Choosing the Right Tools

There are so many ways to cut this joint that one big obstacle to mastering it is choosing a technique. I've tried many ways to cut this joint – backsaws, commercial table-saw tenon jigs and even the sweet Leigh Frame Mortise and Tenon Jig.

Each technique or jig has advantages in economy, speed or accuracy. The technique I'm outlining here is the one I keep coming back to year after year. It uses three tools: a hollow-chisel

mortiser for the mortises, a dado stack to cut the tenons and a shoulder plane to fine-tune your joints. Yes, this is a little bit of an investment, but once you start using this technique, these tools will become the foundation for much of your joint-making.

• *Hollow-chisel mortisers:* These machines are nothing new, but the benchtop ones are now cheaper, more powerful and more accurate than ever. For about $400, you'll get a good machine.

Essentially, a mortiser is a marriage between a drill press and an arbor press that's designed for metalworking. The drill press part has a spinning chuck that holds an auger bit that chews up the waste wood. The auger bit is encased in a hollow four-sided chisel that cleans up the walls of your mortise, making the auger's round hole a square one.

The arbor press part of the machine

Hollow-chisel mortisers excel at boring square holes. Here you can see the holddown (which is usually inadequate with other machines), the table (which must be squared to the chisel before use) and the lever (which makes the machine plow through almost any job).

is the gear-and-lever system that pushes the tooling into your wood. This mechanism gives you an enormous mechanical advantage compared to outfitting your drill press with a mortising attachment – an accessory I don't recommend for all but the most occasional mortising jobs.

Shopping for the proper mortiser is tough. I don't consider all the machines equal. Some are weak and stall in difficult woods such as oak, ash and maple. Many have problems holding your work down against the machine's table. In most cases I prefer fast machines (3,450 rpm) to slow machines (1,750-rpm). The fast machines are almost impossible to stall. However, the marketplace seems to prefer the slow machines.

• *Dado stack:* A good dado stack will serve you in many ways, but I use mine mostly for cutting tenons and rabbets. When it comes to choosing one, buy a set with 8" blades instead of 6" blades, unless you own a benchtop table saw.

Stay away from the bargain sets that cost $50 or less – I haven't found them to be very sharp and the teeth aren't well-ground. The expensive sets ($200 and more) are nice, but they're probably more than you need unless you are making your living at woodworking. My favorite mid-priced set is the Freud SD208. It's about $100 and does a fine job.

• *Shoulder plane:* No matter how accurately you set up your machines to cut mortises and tenons, some will need a little tuning up before assembly. And nothing trims a tenon as well as a shoulder plane. These hand tools really are secret weapons when it comes to joints that fit together firmly and are airtight.

Why is that? Well, shoulder planes are designed to take a controlled shaving that can be as thin as .001". I can tweak a tenon to a perfect fit with just a few passes. Trying to tweak a tenon with a chisel or sandpaper is more difficult. You are more likely to gouge or round over the surface of your tenon and compromise its mechanical strength.

Buying a shoulder plane gets easier every year because there are now many quality tools on the market. Unless you build only small projects, you are going to want a plane that is at least 1" wide. Most casework tenons are 1" long, so a 1"-wide plane is perfect for trimming up the face cheeks and shoulders of the tenon.

My advice is to stay away from the newly made Stanley shoulder planes. I've had some sloppily made Stanleys go though my hands (vintage Stanley shoulder planes can be good, however).

Lie-Nielsen makes two shoulder-trimming planes worth saving your money for. The #073 is a tool of great mass and presence and does the job admirably – it's a $250 investment. Lie-Nielsen also makes a rabbeting block plane that can be easily used as a shoulder plane; it costs $175. It's the tool I recommend to most people because it does double-duty as a low-angle block plane.

Veritas, the tool line made by Lee Valley Tools, has three sizes of shoulder plane that are quite comfortable to use and reasonably priced depending on size from $179-$235. Other new and vintage

A shoulder plane tweaks tenons to fit perfectly. Avoid the modern Stanley shoulder planes (not shown). Spending a few dollars more will get you a much better tool.

brand names worth checking out include Shepherd Tool (made in Canada) and the British-made Clifton, Record, Preston, Spiers and Norris.

Designing a Joint

Once you have the tools you need, you can learn about the mechanics of the joint. Study the illustration on the top of page 29 to learn what each part of the joint is called.

The first question beginners always ask is: How thick and how long should my tenons be? As far as thickness goes, the rule of thumb is that they should be one-half the thickness of your workpiece. So a tenon on a piece of ¾" material should be ⅜" thick.

As for length, that depends on your project. Typical casework tenons that are 1" long will be plenty strong. For large glass doors, make them 1¼" long. For small lightweight frames and doors, stick with ¾"- or ⅝"-long tenons.

What beginners often don't ask about is the size of the edge shoulders on their tenons. This is a critical measurement. If you make these edge shoulders too small, say ³⁄₁₆" wide or so, you could run into huge problems at assembly time when building frames and doors.

Here's why: If your tenoned piece forms one of the outside members of a frame, your mortise wall is going to be only ³⁄₁₆" wide and it's going to be weak. The hydraulic pressure from the glue or

the smallest amount of racking will cause the tenon to blow out this weak mortise wall, ruining everything. It is because of this that I recommend edge shoulders that are ⅜" wide in most cases. Note that your edge shoulders can be too big. Once they start getting larger than ½", you run the risk of allowing the work to twist or warp in time, ruining the alignment of the parts.

Of course, if your tenoned piece is not on the edge of a frame, you can have narrow edge shoulders without any worries.

Designing the mortise is a bit simpler. It should be the same dimensions as your tenon with one exception: Make the mortise ¹⁄₁₆" deeper than your tenon is long. This extra depth does two things: It gives your excess glue a place to go and it ensures your tenon won't bottom out in the mortise, which would prevent you from getting a gap-free joint.

Beware of other tune-ups that some books and magazines suggest. One bit of common advice is to chamfer all the sharp edges of your tenons to improve the fit. Another bit of advice is to chamfer the entry hole of the mortise. These are unnecessary if you design your joint properly.

One thing that is important, however, is to mark the outside faces on all your parts. It's important to keep these straight during machining and assembly.

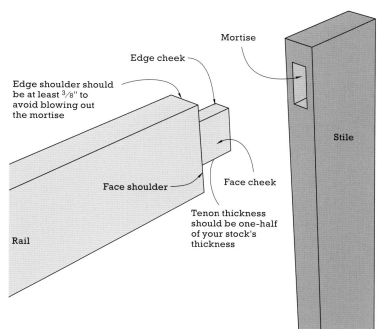

Edge shoulder should be at least 3/8" to avoid blowing out the mortise

Edge cheek

Mortise

Stile

Face shoulder

Face cheek

Rail

Tenon thickness should be one-half of your stock's thickness

These sample mortises are useful for sizing your tenons. I usually make a new one every season or two, because they can get worn from use.

Tenons First

Some traditional woodworkers tell you to make all your mortises first and then make your tenons fit that. This is good advice if you cut the joint by hand with a backsaw and a mortising chisel because there is more opportunity for the mortise to be irregular in size. But you will work much faster and with much less measuring if you try it my way.

Before you cut your first tenon, you should fire up the hollow-chisel mortiser and make a sample mortise with each size of bit you use. The three most common sizes are ¼", ⅜" and ½". These mortises should have perfectly square walls and be 1⅟₁₆" deep and 2" long. Write the month and year on each mortise and make a new set next season.

Why make these sample mortises? Well, because the tooling to make your mortises will always produce the same width mortise, you can merely size all your tenons to one of these sample mortises as you cut them on your table saw. This will save you time down the road, as you'll see.

With your sample mortise in hand, set up your table saw to cut your tenons. Install the dado stack blades and chippers on the saw's arbor. The rule here is to install enough blades to almost cut the length of the tenon in one pass. For example, to cut a 1"-long tenon, set up

enough blades and chippers to make a ¾"-wide cut.

Next, position your saw's rip fence. Measure from the left-most tooth of your dado stack to the fence and shoot for the exact length of your tenon. A 1"-long tenon should measure 1" from the left-most tooth to the fence, as shown in the photo below.

Get your slot miter gauge out and square the fence or head of the gauge to the bar that travels in the table saw's slot. Attach a wooden fence to the face of the gauge (usually this involves screws

through holes already drilled in the gauge). This wooden fence stabilizes your workpiece and controls tear-out as the dado stack blades exit the cut.

Set the height of the blades to just a little shy of the shoulder cut you're after. You want to sneak up on the perfect setting by raising the arbor of the saw instead of lowering it. This does two things: One, it produces fewer waste pieces that result from overshooting your mark. And two, because of the mechanical backlash inherent in all geared systems such as your table saw,

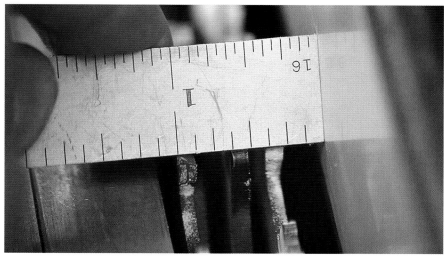

A 6" rule will help you set the length of your tenon. Once you do this a couple of times you'll hit this measurement right away every time.

When making tenons with a dado stack in your table saw, the first pass should remove the bulk of the material. Keep firm downward pressure on your work, which will give you more accurate cuts.

Backing board

No wood trapped between blades and fence

The second pass has the work against the fence and defines the face shoulder. Note there isn't any wood between the fence and blades, so the chance of kickback is minimal. The backing board reduces the chance of tear-out at the shoulders.

Cut the edge shoulders the same way you cut the face shoulders and cheeks.

raising the arbor eliminates any potential for it to slip downward because of backlash.

You are now ready to make a test cut. First put a scrap piece up against your miter gauge, turn on the saw and make a cut on the end of the board. Use firm downward pressure on the piece. Don't let the end of the board touch the saw's rip fence. Then bring the scrap piece and miter gauge back and make a second pass, this time with the scrap touching the rip fence as shown above.

Flip the scrap over and repeat the process on the other face. Usually you aren't supposed to use your rip fence and miter gauge in tandem, but this is an exception. This cut is safe because there isn't any waste that could get trapped between the blades and the fence, producing a kickback.

Check your work with your dial calipers and see if the tenon will fit your sample mortise. The tenon is likely going to be too thick. Raise the blades just a bit and take passes on both faces of the scrap until the tenon fits firmly and snugly into the sample mortise with only hand pressure.

If you can shake the sample mortise and the tenon falls out, you've overshot your mark and need to lower the arbor and try again. If the fit is just a wee bit tight, you can always tune that up with a shoulder plane. Let your dial calipers be your guide. Sometimes you haven't used enough downward pressure during the cut to make a consistent tenon. If something doesn't fit when you know it's supposed to, try making a second pass over the dado stack and push down a little harder during the cut.

Using this setup, mill all the face cheeks on all your tenoned pieces. When that's complete, raise the arbor to ⅜" and use the same routine to cut the edge shoulders on all your boards. Your tenons are now complete.

Use Your Tenons Like a Ruler

One of the major pains in laying out the mortise is figuring out exactly where you should bore your hole. You end up adding weirdo measurements and subtracting the measurements of edge shoulders. If you lay out mortise locations using math only, you will make a mistake someday.

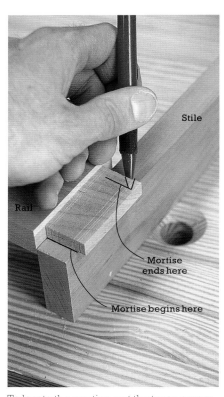

Stile

Rail

Mortise ends here

Mortise begins here

To locate the mortise, put the tenon across the edge of the stile where you want your mortise to go. Use a sharp pencil to mark the tenon's location on the edge. Bingo. You've just laid out the mortise's location.

Troy Sexton, one of our contributing editors, showed me this trick one day and I've never done it any other way since. Say you are joining a door rail to a stile – quite a common operation. Simply lay the tenoned rail onto the edge of the stile and line up the edges of both pieces so they're flush. Take a sharp pencil and – using the tenon like a ruler – mark where the tenon begins and ends on the stile. That's it; you've just marked everything you need to know to make your mortise.

If you are placing a rail in the middle of a stile, there is one more step. You'll need to mark on the stile where the edges of the rail should go. Then line up the edge of the rail with that mark and fire away. There's still no addition or subtraction. With all your mortises laid out, you can then get your hollow-chisel mortiser going.

A Finicky Machine

I've used a lot of hollow-chisel mortisers and find them fussy to adjust. Here are some of the important adjustments not covered by some manuals:

• Make sure the chisel is at a perfect 90° angle to the machine's table. I've set up a dozen of these machines and only one has ever been perfect. The solution is to use masking tape to shim between the table and the machine's base.

• Set the proper clearance between the auger bit and the hollow chisel that surrounds it. Some people use the thickness of a dime to set the distance between the tooling. Some people measure. Either way is fine. If the clearance is too little, the machine will jam and the tooling can burn. Too much distance makes a sloppy-bottomed mortise.

• Square the chisel to the fence. The square holes made by the chisel should line up perfectly. If the edges aren't perfectly straight, your chisel isn't square to the fence. Rotate the chisel in its bushing and make sample cuts until everything is perfect.

• Center the chisel so it's cutting in the middle of your workpiece. There might be a clever trick to do this, but I've found that the most reliable method is to make

a test cut and measure the thickness of the mortise's two walls with a dial caliper. When they're the same, your mortise is centered.

Simplify Your Mortising

As you make your mortises, here are a few tips for making things a whole lot easier.

• I like to cut a little wide of the pencil lines that define my mortise. Not much; just 1/32" or so. This extra wiggle room allows you to square up your assembly easier. It doesn't weaken the joint much – most of its strength is in the tenon's face cheeks.

• As you bore your mortises, don't make your holes simply line up one after the other. Make a hole, skip a distance and then make another hole (see the photo below). Then come back and clean up the waste between the two holes. This will greatly reduce the chance of your chisel bending or breaking.

• Keep your chisel and auger lubricated as they heat up. Listen to the sounds your machine makes. As the auger heats up, it can start to rub the inside of the chisel wall and start to screech. Some dry lubricant or a little canning wax squirted or rubbed on the tooling will keep things working during long mortising sessions.

• Finally, make all your mortises with the outside face of the work against the fence. This ensures your parts will line up perfectly during assembly.

Final Tweaks

No matter how careful you have been, some of your tenons might fit a little too tightly. This is where the shoulder plane shines. Make a couple of passes on both face cheeks and try fitting the joint again. Be sure to make the same number of passes on each cheek to keep the tenon centered on the rail. If your parts aren't in the same plane when assembled (and they're supposed to be), you can take passes on only one cheek to try to make corrections.

If the joint closes up on one face but not the other, you might have a sloppy shoulder. The shoulder plane can trim the fat shoulder to bring it in line with its twin on the other side of the tenon. If the tenon still won't seat tightly, try chiseling out some meat at the corner where the edge shoulder meets the face cheek – but don't trim the outside edge of the edge shoulder itself.

Finally, get a sharp chisel and clean out any gunk at the bottom of the mortise. Keep at it – a tight joint is worth the extra effort.

Assembly

You really don't want any glue squeeze-out when you assemble your mortise-and-tenon joints. The trick to this is learning where to put the glue and how much to use. I run a thick bead of glue at the top of each mortise wall and then paint the inside of the mortise wall with glue using a little scrap piece. I try to

Line marked on stile

Mortise is cut slightly past that line

By cutting over your line slightly, you give yourself just enough forgiveness at assembly time. A little wiggle can mean a lot when you are trying to close up the gaps as you clamp up your work.

leave the glue a little thick at the top of the mortise wall. Then, when the tenon is inserted, this paints the tenon with glue but drives the excess to the bottom of the mortise.

When clamping any frame – regardless of the joinery you used – you don't want to use too much pressure or you will distort the frame. Tighten the clamps until the joints close and no more. You also want to alternate your clamps over and under the assembly to keep the frame flat – no matter how fancy your clamps are.

Once you do this a couple of times, I think you'll find a whole new level of woodworking open to you. Web frames for dressers (or Chippendale secretaries) will seem like no problem. Morris chairs with 112 mortises will be within your reach. And your furniture is more likely to stand the test of time – and maybe even the occasional anvil.

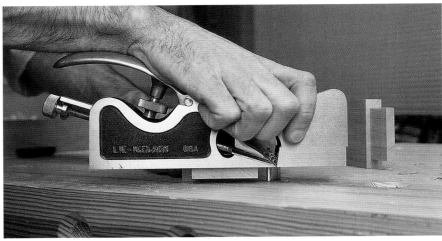

Shoulder planes are capable of extraordinarily precise work. Just try to set your table saw to remove .001". It's not possible. For a shoulder plane, it's simple.

A thick bead of glue at the top of the mortise wall makes the joint strong without squeezing out a lot of glue. Use a small piece of scrap to paint the mortise wall before inserting the tenon.

Dovetails

BY FRANK KLAUSZ

The dovetail is an ancient joint widely used in cathedrals, barns and Egyptian furniture. It is the right joint for many items including fine furniture, carcases, drawers and jewelry boxes. They are all dovetailed together.

I was only 27 years old when I came to this country in 1968 from my native Hungary. Although I had a piece of paper that said "master cabinetmaker," I was still very eager to learn more about my trade.

Where I came from I was happy if I could carry a white-haired master's tool chest to the job site because I knew I would learn a thing or two that day working with him. Now I am that white-haired master with 45 years of experience in the trade.

In the early 1970s I went to a lot of seminars. Some were on dovetailing with well-known teachers in the woodworking world. Some cut the tails first; others cut the pins first. They used tools that I didn't own, such as a dovetail marker. They measured the size of the pins and tails, which is completely different from my method. The more I studied, the more confused I became. I decided to find the best way to cut tight dovetails quickly.

A Search for the Best Method

I owned an antique restoration shop. I had a chance to study a lot of antiques from around the world. Each time a piece of furniture came to the shop, the first thing I looked at was the dovetails. I studied hundreds of them and made tracings of dozens of unusual pieces. I tried to find an answer for my methods. I learned in Hungary, I worked in Vienna, and I was looking for someone from a different part of the world than Eastern Europe to do dovetails. I found Hector, from Guatemala, a master cabinetmaker.

"This is great, Central America!" I said. I asked him to make me dovetails. He said, "You cabinetmaker, you make dovetail." We had a language problem. I had a hard time explaining to him my intentions. I replied, "I know how to cut dovetails, I want to see how you do it." "OK," he said. He grabbed some chisels, a dovetail saw, a marking gauge, some scrap wood, set up the marking gauge to the thickness of the wood, marked the

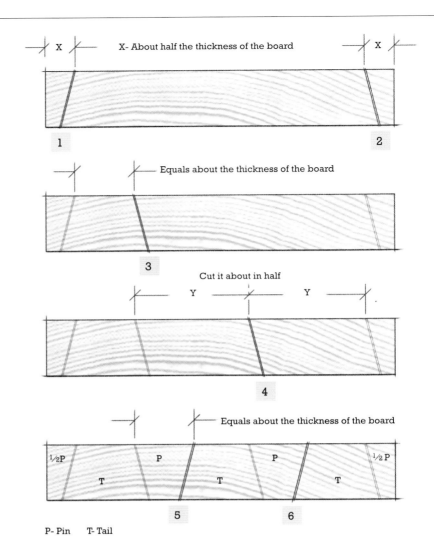

X- About half the thickness of the board

Equals about the thickness of the board

Cut it about in half

Equals about the thickness of the board

½P   P   P   ½P

T   T   T

P- Pin   T- Tail

wood, clamped it into a vise and started cutting. He cut the pins, chiseled the pins; from the pins he marked the tails, chiseled the tails and put it together. "How is that?" he asked. I was as happy as can be! "That is exactly the way I do it," I replied.

After my experience with Hector, and my 10 years of researching dovetail techniques, I came to the conclusion that Grandpa wasn't a bad craftsman at all and my father taught me well.

Later on, I wrote some articles for different magazines and I made some videos – one of them is "Dovetail a Drawer with Frank Klausz." Before I knew it, I was teaching the craft throughout America. I taught hundreds of people how to dovetail. A lesson took plus or minus one hour with a 99 percent student success rate (let's face it, some of us are born with two left hands).

Anyone Can Do It

If you already know how to do dovetails, and are happy with your method, I am happy for you and don't mean to change your ways. If you are a beginner or learning about new methods, you can do it my way. I know you can do it!

How do you know how to write? You learned in school. You made a whole row of a's. You made a whole row of b's. Before you knew it, you were writing words and sentences. That's how I learned to do dovetails. In school, I cut a whole row of straight cuts without marking, checked it often with a square, and improved the next row. In the next lesson, I cut angles approximately 10° to 15°, all to the left, the next row all to the right, and before I knew it, I was cutting dovetails.

Companies sell router bits from 7° to 18°, so the angle you use is a personal choice. The strongest dovetails have equal-sized pins and tails, like machine-made drawers. Pope John Paul II's coffin had approximately 3" pins and 3" tails. The choices are endless.

Cutting Dovetails My Way

So how do you make dovetails my way? Make yourself a cheat sheet (see the drawing on page 34) or look at some dovetails to copy. Get some scrap wood. Mill them to the same size: 3½" to 4" wide, ½" thick and cut them 5" to 6" long. Mill five, 10 pieces, whatever it takes. Set up your marking gauge exactly to the thickness of the wood. Mark the face of the wood. Clamp it into your bench vise, and start cutting with your dovetail saw. (I hope you already practiced your rows of straight and angled cuts.)

Every dovetail starts with a half pin. On the other side is another half pin. Cut them. Next to the half pin you need a full tail. Cut it. Cut the remaining distance in half with the same angle, turn it around, make two more cuts and you're done. Cut only pins, and cut as many as you need until you are pleased.

There's no marking involved – use your eyesight and judgment, and use the thickness of the wood for the width of the tails by judging distances. Make them to your liking. My pins are a little smaller than the tails. That's the way I like them. You may make them the same way or you may make small pins such as ones found in English furniture. They are all good. You are cutting hand-cut dovetails; there should be some variation. Hand-cut dovetails have character and Mrs. Jones likes that.

Once you're happy with your pins, chisel the pins. Put the chisel on the marking gauge line and tap it. Take out a little "V" cut. Now chisel deeper, taking out chips. Undercut just a very little. Flip the piece over and do the same on the other side.

Next, use your pins to make the tails. Hold all three sides even with the edge and the end. With a sharp pencil, mark it from the inside. Here is the hard part: When you cut the pins a little this way or a little that way, it doesn't matter because you're making a template. But when you cut the tails, you have to be accurate and cut that pencil line in half. To understand

Cutting Dovetails the Klausz Way

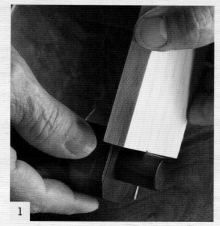

Set up the marking gauge exactly to the thickness of the wood.

Next, mark the wood.

Cut a half pin.

Cut another half pin.

which side of the pencil line you are cutting, you have to mark the half pins and pins with an "X." That will be your waste. When you chisel out your waste, the "X" will become sawdust and chips. Cut off your half pins; chisel your tails (you are chiseling out the space for the pins).

Here comes the fun part: Try fitting it together. If it doesn't fit, try to find out why, but don't fix it. Cut your next piece. You may have to go closer to the line if it is too tight or leave more of the line on to make it tighter. Make a new one using the same pins until you are happy with a snug fit.

You are ready to make a jewelry box for your mother-in-law. Good luck trying, I am sure you can do it! Happy woodworking.

Cut Dovetails Easily on Bigger Boards

When cutting dovetails on a wider board, use the same method as I describe in this chapter. You have to divide the remaining space after your third cut in half and half again, or $1/3$. With practice it will come naturally. The thicker the wood, the bigger the pins and tails. For example, a 1"-thick board for a blanket chest should have 1" to $1\frac{1}{2}$" tails. It both looks good and is very strong. When I was an apprentice watching my father work, I asked him, "How can you do this so fast?" He replied, "Don't worry, after 10 to 15 years you will be a good beginner yourself."

5

Cut a tail.

6

Divide the distance in half between the two saw kerfs and cut it.

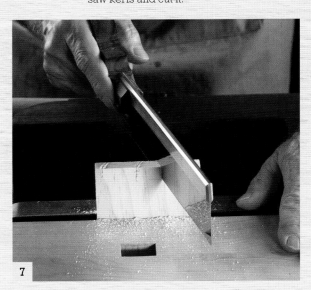

Go back to your first angle and cut another pin.

7

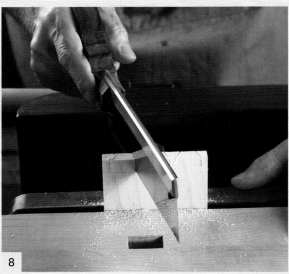

Cut one more pin. You're done cutting pins.

8

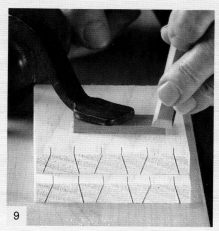

9

Put the chisel into the marking gauge line and tap it.

10

Do the same on all the tails.

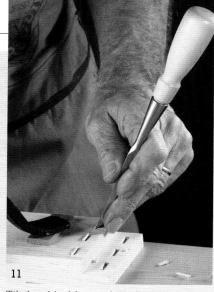

11

Tilt the chisel forward to take out a little piece.

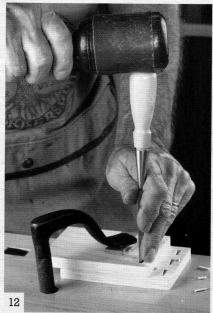

12

Put the chisel back up and tap it more. Undercut a little bit, approximately 2°.

13

With a smaller chisel, chisel into the corners. Chisel about halfway.

14

Flip your stock and chisel from the other side.

15

From the pins, mark the tails. Hold the pin board flush on the outside and on the edges.

16

Mark your waste (the bits of wood you will be cutting out) with an "X."

17

Line up your saw with the pencil line. Use your thumb for a guide and cut on the "X" side.

18

Here you can see what it looks like to leave the lines on the tails.

19

Cut off the half pin. The saw kerf should be outside of the marking gauge line.

20

Chisel the tails the same way you chiseled the pins.

21

With the edge of your chisel, push out your waste.

22

If you did everything right, it should easily tap together.

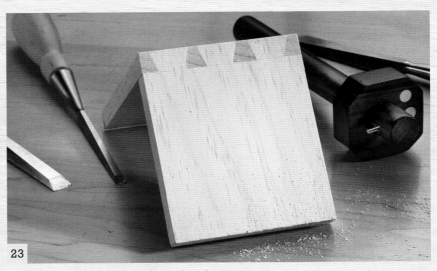

23

Here you can see the finished practice piece.

Tapered Sliding Dovetails

BY FRANK STRAZZA

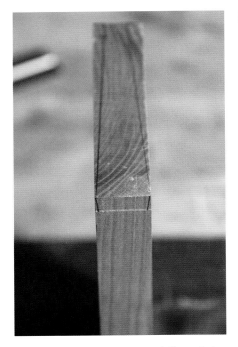

I use a dovetail saw to make the tapered cuts; notice how I use thumb pressure against the saw to keep it correctly aligned to the cut.

Use a chisel to create a "wall" against which you can register your saw.

After marking the baseline at $1/4$", mark the taper on the end grain.

First, mark the small end of the tail. (Note that your knife position is critical here, and be sure to mark both sides.) Then mark the wide end on the other edge of the pin board.

Tapered sliding dovetails are multipurpose joints traditionally used for drawer dividers, holding legs in place on a pedestal table and attaching tops to case pieces.

The primary reason for a tapered joint (instead of a straight joint) is the reduced friction over its length. The tapered sliding dovetail gets tight only during the final fit, when it is ready to seat home. This reduced friction makes fitting much easier.

Once the joint is seated, it is extremely tight and often requires no glue. Hand-cutting this joint is easier and quicker than the lengthy process of setting up a jig and machine.

After incorporating tapered joints into much of my furniture, I've found them strong and multifunctional; I believe you'll enjoy their benefits, as well as the challenge of cutting the joint, as much as I have.

I'll show you how to create a small tapered sliding dovetail, such as would be used for a drawer divider.

Tail Layout

For this exercise, I use two ¾"-thick x 4"-wide cherry boards (a typical size for a drawer divider).

The first step is to cut the tapered tail (after making sure that the end of your board is perfectly square).

Set a cutting gauge (not a pinned marking gauge, which would tear the fibers rather than cutting them) to ¼" and scribe all around the end of the tail board to mark the baseline. On the board's edge, the sliding dovetail appears identical to a regular dovetail. However, from above, there will be a taper.

Place the tail board upright in your vise in preparation for marking tapered lines on the end grain. Starting with the end facing you, place a straightedge on the outside edge. Angle it toward the other end of the board, with a slope of about one-quarter the thickness of the board; in this case, that will be ³⁄₁₆". Draw a tapered line with a pencil along the straightedge. Repeat this process for the opposing side.

Using a dovetail marker or bevel gauge, draw the lines for the tail on the edge of the board. (I like a 1:7 angle.)

Cut the Tail

Cutting the angles on the top is a bit of a challenge, but no more than sawing a tenon cheek. Starting at the back, cut partway down your line, shift the saw to the front and make another partial cut, then join the two cuts. It is helpful to apply pressure between your thumb and the side of the saw to keep it aligned.

It's important that the two tapers on the end grain are straight and that the angles that make up the tail are cut accurately. Remember – you are only cutting down ¼".

Cut the Shoulder

With a knife, deepen the shoulder line that you marked with your cutting gauge.

Now use a chisel to create a wall right against the knifed line. That creates a nice shoulder to set your saw against to use as a guide for accurate cutting. (This method is effective for extreme accuracy in cross-grain cuts.) But don't overcut! Inspect the tail to ensure that the shoulders are crisp and clean.

On occasion, I use a sliding dovetail plane to cut the tail, but I've found it not as effective for a narrow tail such as this one. (However, if you're creating a long sliding dovetail, such as on a tabletop, the plane is essential.)

Mark & Cut the Pin

The next step is to transfer the tail to the pin. Mark two pencil lines square across the pin board to indicate the width (¾") and placement of the tail board. Draw a face mark on the inside of your pin board on the right-hand side and another one on the right-hand side of the tail board. These marks should face each other; they will help you keep the alignment correct.

Lay your tail board on edge with the small dovetail end touching the pin board, with the end grain facing you. With your knife closest to the shoulder, mark the small end of the tail on both

sides. Now flip the tail board end to end so the end grain faces away from you. Mark the large end of the tail on the edge of the pin board closest to you, marking both sides right at the shoulder.

The key is transferring an image of the narrow section of the tail onto the pin board.

With a straightedge, join the marks for both tapers front to back. Then with a knife, lightly scribe along the straightedge. Remove the straightedge and go over the knife cuts several times to deepen the lines.

Transfer the 1:7 angles of the tail onto the edge of the pin board.

Using the same ¼" setting on your cutting gauge, mark the depth of the pin recess.

As you did for the shoulder cuts, use a chisel in your layout lines to create a wall for your saw to follow, then saw down the length of the taper line, carefully following the angle of the tail. Be sure not to overcut.

Working from both sides, remove the waste using a ⅜" and a ¼" chisel, with the bevels facing up.

With a small router plane, remove any excess material, bringing an even depth to the floor of the pin.

Now the moment of truth! Slide the tail into the socket and use a hammer to

seat it tightly. If it's too tight and doesn't go all the way home, that's a good problem. Look at both ends, and you can usually tell where the problem lies. If it's too tight on one end, simply chisel away the material on the pin board. (If it's too loose, start over with a fresh pin board.)

And don't worry if your joint isn't perfect on the first try; it took me several practice sessions the first time, too.

Now slide the tail into its socket; use a hammer to knock it home.

The finished sliding dovetail joint should seat firmly in place. If you've cut it perfectly, you don't even need glue.

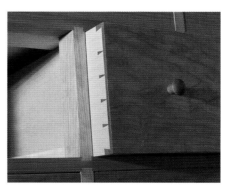

The tapered sliding dovetail is my joint of choice to divide casework drawers.

Work in from both sides to remove the waste. On the wider side, a ³⁄₈" chisel is the best choice; working from the narrower side, switch to a ¹⁄₄"-wide tool.

Level the floor of the socket using a small router plane.

10 Tricks for Tight Joints

Y ou've cut all your pieces and are putting everything together when you first notice it – a gap. A dark void where there should be none.

Don't panic – it happens to the best of us. For whatever reason, there are instances when your joints just don't fit perfectly and you have to decide what to do: Do you scrap all the time, energy, money and hard work you've put into the project and start over, or do you just let there be a little gap and move on?

Well, we're giving you a third option. We put our heads together and have come up with a list of the best tricks to help you tighten your joints. These tips should help you eliminate those unsightly, embarrassing gaps and point your joints in the right direction.

Compression Makes Dovetails Tight

Hand-cut dovetails are some of the most challenging joints to fit perfectly. Many woodworkers will spend hundreds of dollars on router jigs or woodworking classes to get an airtight fit.

If you decide to hand-cut your dovetails, there are a few ways to make sure you get it right.

Because wood is – on a cellular level – similar to a bunch of soda straws glued together, you can compress it a little bit. Usually, compression is a bad thing, such as when you drop a hammer on your work and it dents. But a little bit of compression is good when dovetailing.

Here's how it works: Cut the first half of your joint as you usually would – I usually cut the tails first. Then use that first half to knife in the second half of the joint – in this case, the pins.

Next, when you saw your pin lines, don't saw right up against the knife line you marked, as most books tell you. Instead, saw slightly wide. How wide? The whisker of a gnat would be a good place to start. Here's how I do it: After I knife in my joint lines, I run a pencil over each knife line. Then I start my saw cut to leave the entire pencil line.

Like all things pertaining to dovetails, this takes practice. Cut some sample joints to get a feel for it and use a magnifying glass to gauge your progress.

Once you cut your pins, use a knife to ease the inside edges of your tails,

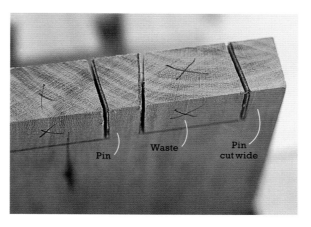

Wood compresses, and you can use that to make your dovetails tighter. Cutting your pins just slightly wide will force them to compress the tails.

which will be inside the joint. When you join your two pieces, the too-tight pins will compress the tails and the joint will be seamless. If you try to compress too much, one of your boards will split as the two boards are knocked together.

This compression works especially well with half-blind drawer joints where you are joining a secondary softwood for the sides (such as poplar) with a hardwood drawer front (such as oak), because the softwood compresses easily. But be careful: This trick doesn't work when you are trying to join two pieces of dense exotic wood, which doesn't compress much at all.

— *Christopher Schwarz*

Fake Half-blinds for Dovetail Joints

Half-blind dovetails are trickier to cut than through-dovetails, but they don't have to be. I picked up this trick from dovetailing maestro Rob Cosman, who has two excellent videos on dovetails that are available from Lie-Nielsen Toolworks (lie-nielsen.com or 800-327-2520).

Essentially, you first build a drawer with the easier through-dovetails and then glue a ¼"-thick piece of veneer over the drawer front, making them look like half-blind dovetails.

Usually with drawers you have ½"-thick sides and a ¾"-thick front. To do what we're suggesting, make your drawer front with ½"-thick stock, too. Then join

Through-dovetails are easier to cut than half-blinds. To make life easier (and to stretch your stock of valuable wood) cut through-dovetails when joining your sides and drawer fronts. Then add ¼"-thick veneer to the drawer front.

the sides to the front using through-dovetails.

Then, using your band saw, resaw a piece of ¼"-thick veneer from a piece of really nice figured wood. Make it a little larger than the finished size of your drawer front. Then glue that veneer to the drawer front, let the glue dry and trim it flush.

This makes excellent half-blind dovetails and allows you to stretch your supply of nicely figured woods for your drawer fronts.

— CS

Deeper Mortises Close Gaps

It's easy to get gaps when using a traditional mortise-and-tenon joint. Luckily, it's also straightforward to get rid of them.

If you make your mortises exactly as deep as your tenons are long, you're asking for trouble. By doing this, you haven't created a place for any excess glue to go, so it will be forced out of the joint. And if there is even a little bit of gunk at the bottom of your mortise, the joint won't close tightly no matter what you do.

To fix this, make your mortises ¹⁄₁₆" deeper than your tenons are long. This trick will save you time because you don't have to clean up the bottoms of your mortises as much, and it will prevent glue from squeezing out if you use too much in the joint.

— CS

Veneered front

Use your workbench as part of your clamping setup when applying the veneer to the drawer. This setup helps spread pressure evenly across this large surface.

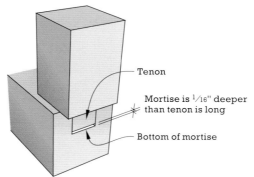

Tenon

Mortise is ¹⁄₁₆" deeper than tenon is long

Bottom of mortise

Making your mortise a little deeper prevents gaps at the shoulders.

Paring Your Shoulders in a Mortise-and-tenon Joint

Before you assemble your joints, you should always clamp them up without glue. That way, you can disassemble everything and fine-tune your joints if you find ugly gaps at this stage. But what if you can't track down the problem? We've found that tuning up the shoulder of the joint will help you fix a variety of problems and make sure you don't hurt the strength of the joint.

First, clamp the tenon in your bench's vise with the tenon pointing straight up. With a sharp chisel, pare away the inside of the shoulder without cutting the outside of the shoulder that shows. Pare away about ⅟₃₂" all the way around and then test the fit again.

This should help you solve problems where your shoulders are angled a bit because of miscutting. It also helps out when the tenon's mating surface isn't perfectly square – it's quite common to sand or plane that area so it's bellied a bit.
— CS

Tighten Mortise-and-tenon Joints with a Shoulder Plane

A common problem with a mortise-and-tenon joint is that it's easy to make the joint too tight (so it won't go together) or too loose (where it will fall apart).

Even expertly machined joints have this problem because it's tough to hold all your parts with exactly the same pressure as you cut them on your table saw or router table. A ⅟₁₂₈" difference can make or break this joint.

Your tenons should slide into your mortises with hand pressure only. The fit should be firm but not forced. To get that every single time, I make all my tenons so they are slightly oversized. Usually I shoot for a tenon that fits a bit too tightly but would go together with a mallet.

Then I get ready for a dry assembly and use my shoulder plane to tune up each joint. A good shoulder plane removes just a couple thousandths of an inch in a pass. This allows you to sneak up on a brilliant fit with only five or six swipes of the plane. It takes about 10 seconds per joint.

Be sure to remove the same amount of material from each face cheek of the tenon by taking the same number of passes on each side of the tenon.

Shoulder planes are available new from Lie-Nielsen, Clifton, Stanley and some other custom plane-makers, such as Shepherd Tool. You also can find them at flea markets or on the Internet.
— CS

Add Rabbets to Dado Joints

Dados are deceivingly simple: You just cut a trench in your work that is exactly the same width as the thickness of its mating piece.

The problem is getting the dado sized exactly right so you don't have an ugly

Pare the shoulder all around the tenon to help eliminate gaps in this joint. Be sure not to cut the edge of the shoulder, or you'll make your gap worse instead of better.

gap at the front of your joint or along the trench where the boards meet. Of course, to precisely size your dados you can use shims in your dado stack, buy undersized router bits or cut your joint in a couple of passes.

Another option is to cut a rabbet on the mating piece. Using a rabbet requires an extra machinery setup, but it is worth the trouble. Cut your dado so its width is ⅛" undersized. For example, if you were planning on a ¾"-wide dado, make a ⅝"-wide dado instead.

Then cut an ⅛"-deep rabbet on your mating piece that allows the two pieces to nest together. You can tweak the size of the rabbet to get the joint just right.
— Steve Shanesy

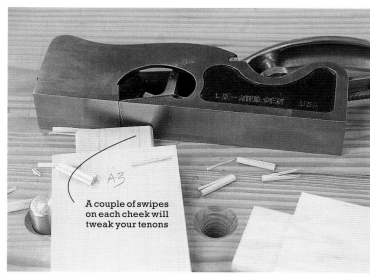

To get your tenons fitting perfectly, learn to use a shoulder plane. This handy tool will fit your tenons in an extraordinarily controlled manner.

Dados are a pain to get sized just right. So don't bother sizing the dado to the material. Cut the dado undersized and then cut a matching rabbet on its mate.

Use a Hand Plane for Dados

Another way to get perfect dados is with the help of a smoothing plane. If you can sharpen and set up a plane, this is for you.

First, cut your dado so it is slightly undersized. I've found that the dado made by dado stacks is always a few thousandths of an inch less than the width you require. To cut a slightly undersized ¾"-wide dado, I merely install all the chippers for a ¾" dado. This has always worked, regardless of the brand of dado stack (Forrest, Freud and others).

Then I just plane down the mating piece on both sides to sneak up on a perfect fit. Make sure you set your plane to make the finest shaving possible, and this should work for you.

— CS

Stop Bridging Your Screws When Using Butt Joints

There definitely are ways to improve your butt joints if you find gaps appearing. Screws and biscuits – used correctly – can make the joint tighter and more durable if you know how to use them.

While dovetails and mortise-and-tenon joints are excellent options, we know that a lot of woodworkers use screws to simply pull butt joints tight. There's nothing wrong with that, but using the correct screws and techniques will ensure that your joint actually is tight.

Lots of woodworkers are using sheet-metal screws and drywall screws to assemble projects. These will work, but there's a reason woodworking screws exist.

The thread-free part of a wood screw shank (under the screw head) allows the threads to bite into the second wood piece, while the first piece (the one being attached) is able to pull tight against it. If there are threads over the entire length of the screw shank, the threads will bite into the wood in the attaching piece and will stop the first piece from seating tight when the screw head reaches the wood surface. This is something called "bridging," and you'll never get a tight joint.

Using a standard wood screw with a partially-threaded shank will solve this, or you can make sure the clearance hole in the attaching piece is large enough to keep the threads from catching in the wood. Either way, your joint will end up tight and solid.

— David Thiel

Improve Butt Joints with Pocket-hole Screws, Biscuits

We like pocket-hole screws to build utility cabinets and frames because no other joint is as fast or requires as little clamping.

But there is one downside with pocket-hole screws when you are joining a shelf, top or bottom to a side. It can be quite difficult to hold the shelf in perfect position as you drive the screws home. If the piece shifts even the slightest bit, you'll have a shelf that is cockeyed with an ugly, obvious gap on one side.

To get around this, we combine biscuits and pocket-hole screws to get the best of both worlds. The extra time the biscuits take is minimal. First, cut your biscuit slots in your shelf and side piece. Then cut the pocket holes in the underside of the shelf.

Put glue and biscuits in the biscuit slots and put the shelf in place. Then you can drive the pocket-hole screws home. Why do we like this method so much? Well, there are three reasons:

• The biscuits hold the shelf in place as you drive the screws so it cannot shift and your case will be perfectly square.

• The pocket-hole screws hold the

A sharp and tuned smoothing plane can reduce your thickness in small increments, allowing you to sneak up on a seamless dado joint.

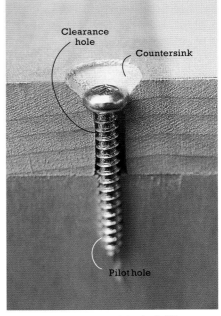

Clearance hole

Countersink

Pilot hole

The trick to a tight butt joint is drilling a proper clearance hole before you drive in a sheet-metal screw. The clearance hole prevents the threads from catching in the top piece.

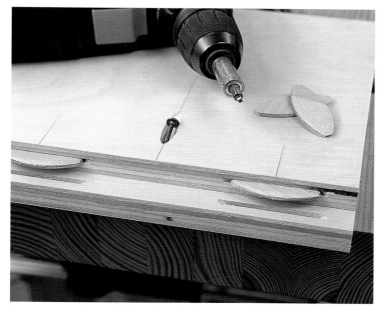

Biscuits keep the shelf aligned vertically and the pocket-hole screws help clamp the middle of the panel. Add some glue, cinch the screws down tight and you're done – it's that easy. And here's the best part: No clamps required.

When taping your miters, lay the parts face up so the mitered edges are touching. Then tape the joint with clear packing tape.

shelf and side pieces together as the glue dries. This is especially helpful with the middle part of the shelf, which is difficult to clamp if you use only biscuits. The pocket-hole screws pull the pieces together across the shelf without a single clamp.

• If you are a cheapskate, you can remove the screws once the glue is dry and reuse them.

— CS

The Best Way to Clamp Miters in Casework

Joining your cabinet's sides and face frame with a miter is a classy way to dress up an ordinary box – and it is a signature of contemporary furniture design. But accomplishing this joint without an ugly gap somewhere along that miter is another story.

Many people spend lots of money on corner clamps and clamping jigs. Or they construct convoluted cauls. My solution is tape. Yes, tape.

I was shown this technique of cutting straight and clean joints and taping them together when I worked in a large production cabinet shop where time was money. I've used this technique on mitered joints that were 10' long and it worked flawlessly. It also works great for gluing compound miters.

To cut a clean miter using your table saw, set the blade to 45° and clamp an accessory fence to your saw's rip fence. The accessory fence should be made using a softer wood, such as poplar or pine. A harder wood will ruin the sharp tip of your miter. Raise the blade while it is spinning until it kisses the accessory fence. Now you can cut your miters.

The real trick to dead-on miters is how you glue them. As shown in the photos, tape the outside of the joint together, spread glue on the joint and then fold the parts to assemble things. Band clamps or more tape will hold the parts together as they dry.

— Jim Stack

Next fold the assembly and use tape to hold it square until the glue sets.

Tall Chest: Carcase Construction

BY LONNIE BIRD

If you've never tried your hand at building a chest of drawers but you've built several projects with success, the simple tall chest in this chapter is a good place to begin. Because of its scale, a chest of drawers can seem intimidating at first glance. But stripped of its feet and moulding, this chest, like all chests, is just a box. And of course the drawers are simply boxes, too, which are made to fit within the large box.

The key to building casework is to make it square. Otherwise, as you can imagine, it becomes very difficult to fit the drawers and mouldings. The key to making the casework square is to use a stop-block when cutting parts to final length. Remember, for the corners of a box to be 90°, or square, parallel parts must be the exact same length. If you measure, mark and cut parallel parts separately they probably will not be exactly the same length. Instead, if you measure and mark just one piece and set up a stop-block, the mating parts will be identical.

Once the basic case is constructed there is no longer a need to measure. Instead, the remaining parts of the case, such as drawers and moulding, are marked directly from the case. Using these tested techniques not only ensures that the parts fit, the construction process is much more efficient as well.

Chests of drawers such as the one shown at left were very popular two cen-turies ago in the New England Colonies. I like them for their simplicity. They rely on good proportions and careful selection of figured wood rather than lots of curves and carvings; this chest fits within a golden rectangle and the drawers gradu-ate using arithmetic progression. The casework is supported by tall bracket feet, which were common on New England chests of this classic period. And capping off the chest is a bold crown moulding.

Many of the surviving antique chests are made from tiger maple; a few are crafted of cherry. Tiger maple is one of my favorite woods but I opted for cherry because I had some special planks that I cut and dried myself. The case sides and top are made from a matching set of 22"-wide boards. As you can imagine it was a large, old tree. In fact, it was so old that the base of the tree was beginning to rot and so the commercial mills just were not interested in the tree. It's a good example of what you can often find when you develop rapport with a professional logger. Finding lumber like this at a lum-beryard is difficult to impossible.

One-board sides and a top are dra-matic, but two well-matched boards look great, too. And the specialty lumber deal-ers in Pennsylvania often have wide, fig-ured boards in stock. So gather the nec-essary materials, sharpen your chisels, grab your dovetail saw and let's begin.

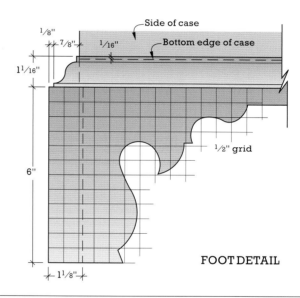

FOOT DETAIL

Tall Chest: Carcase Construction

NO.	ITEM	DIMENSIONS (INCHES)			MATERIAL
		T	W	L	
2	Sides	7/8	19	46	Cherry
1	Top	7/8	19	31	Cherry
1	Bottom	7/8	18	31	Poplar
1	Bottom edging	1/2	7/8	31	Cherry
1	Front foot	7/8	6	33 1/2	Cherry
2	Side feet	1 1/8	6	20	Cherry
2	Back support blocks	7/8	6	12	Poplar
2	Base frame	7/8	2	31 1/2	Poplar
2	Base frame	7/8	2	17	Poplar
7	Dividers	7/8	2	30 1/2	Cherry
7	Dividers	7/8	2	30 1/2	Poplar
14	Drawer runners	7/8	1 3/4	16 3/8	Poplar
	Crown moulding	2 1/4	4 1/4	48	Cherry
	Base moulding	1 1/16	4	48	Cherry
	Back	1/2	30	45 7/8	Poplar
	Glue blocks	1/2	1/2	72	Poplar

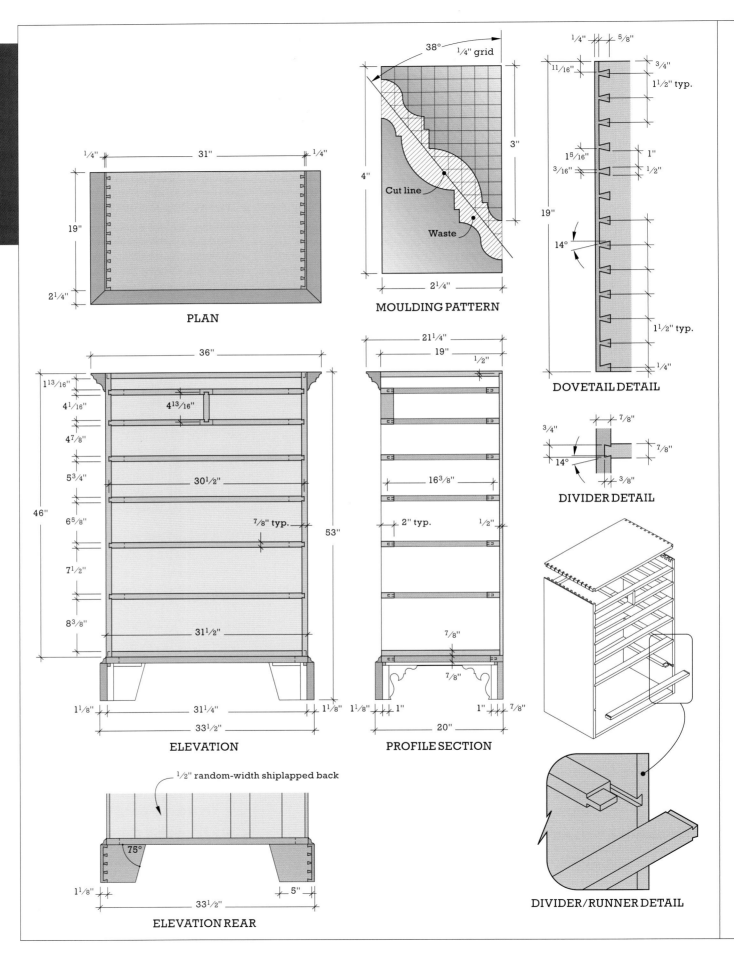

PLAN

MOULDING PATTERN

38°

¼" grid

4"

3"

Cut line

Waste

2¼"

DOVETAIL DETAIL

¼"

5/8"

11/16"

¾"

1½" typ.

1 5/16"

1"

3/16"

½"

19"

14°

1½" typ.

¼"

DIVIDER DETAIL

¾"

7/8"

14°

3/8"

7/8"

ELEVATION

36"

1 13/16"

4 1/16"

4 13/16"

4 7/8"

5¾"

30½"

46"

6 5/8"

7/8" typ.

53"

7½"

8 3/8"

31½"

1 1/8"

31¼"

1 1/8"

33½"

PROFILE SECTION

21¼"

19"

½"

16 3/8"

2" typ.

½"

7/8"

7/8"

1 1/8"

1"

1"

7/8"

20"

DIVIDER/RUNNER DETAIL

½" random-width shiplapped back

75°

1 1/8"

5"

33½"

ELEVATION REAR

Mill the Stock

Before you lay out and cut the first dovetail, it's important to mill the stock flat and square. Cutting dovetails on warped boards is difficult at best. I flatten one face of each board with my jointer before planing the stock to thickness. Afterwards, I square one end of each board and cut the stock to length using a stop-block for accuracy. The stop-block is a critical part of the setup when sawing to final length. For the corners of the chest to be square, the parallel members must be equal in length. Afterward, cut a ½" by ½" rabbet along the inside edges of the sides and top to accept the carcase's backboards.

Dovetail the Box

Once you've milled the four planks for the box, you're ready for joinery. I always use dovetails for furniture casework; no other joint can match the strength and beauty of a row of dovetails. Remember, too, that the chest stands only 53" tall – so the joinery at the top is easily visible; rows of contrasting tails and pins are an eye-catching part of this classic piece of furniture.

It's important to start the layout at the back of the case with a half tail to hide the rabbet. Otherwise, if you begin with a pin, the rabbet will create an ugly void.

Crisp, well-delineated baselines are critical for making a dovetail joint that you'll be proud of. If the marking gauge is sharp, it will incise a crisp layout line as opposed to a line that is torn or ragged. A clean incision will allow you to easily locate the layout line with the chisel edge as you chop the waste areas in the joint. It's a good idea to test the marking gauge in an inconspicuous area and sharpen it if necessary.

For casework such as this chest of drawers, I use half-blind dovetails even though the joint is partially covered by moulding. Remember, solid wood is continually expanding and contracting with the change of seasons. If through dovetails are used, the ends of the tails will push the moulding slightly away from the case during the dry winter months. Half-blind dovetails provide a neat appearance year-round.

Despite what you may have heard, half-blind dovetails are really no more difficult or time-consuming to cut than through dovetails. The technique I use is to cut the waste from between the pins with a router. I don't use a jig. Instead, I lay out the joint carefully with a knife and carefully rout freehand to the layout lines. It may sound difficult, but it's not really; like most woodworking skills it just requires a bit of practice. After routing the waste I chop the rounded, inside corners square with a chisel and mallet. Then I scribe the tails from the pins and saw them by hand. The result is an authentic, hand-cut dovetail joint. The router is used only to efficiently remove the waste from between the pins, which makes the process less tedious and far more efficient. For more on cutting dovetails see the photo essay on page 54.

Assemble the Box

Once all the dovetail joints have been cut and fit, you're ready to assemble the box. To make the glue-up stress-free I first assemble the box and then gently tap each joint halfway open with a mallet to apply the glue. By partially opening the joints I can easily apply the glue and tap the joints closed again; there's no need to match and align mating corners after spreading the glue. I don't use clamps to assemble the case; if the fit is snug the joints will stay closed without clamps. However, if you decide to use clamps, be certain that the clamp pressure doesn't inadvertently twist the case.

Once the joints are assembled, I check the corners for squareness. If the case isn't square, a slight amount of pressure on the acute corners will make it square. I don't use a clamp to square the case. The limited reach of the clamp applies pressure only in a small spot at the clamp head. This causes the box to twist. Instead, I position a corner of the case on the floor of my shop and push gently on the opposite corner. This method applies pressure across the entire depth of the box and easily brings it into square. Now set the box on your bench, undisturbed while the glue dries.

Add the Dividers

After the box is assembled you're ready to construct the interior framework of dividers and runners. There are actually two sets of drawer dividers: one at the case front and one at the back. Each pair is joined by a set of runners with mortises and tenons. The ends of each divider have dovetails, which fit snug within matching dovetailed sockets in the case sides. Once assembled, the dividers and runners create a rigid framework, which adds greatly to the strength and stiffness of the case.

I begin by routing the dovetailed sockets in the case to accept the dividers. To ensure that each divider is square to the case, I use a template to guide the router for corresponding cuts. There's no need to measure because the template registers against the bottom of the case. Besides greatly reducing the amount of time required to cut the sockets, this technique also eliminates potential layout errors. I use a separate template for each set of sockets. This way I'll have the

Template

A plywood template registers against the case bottom to ensure perfect alignment of the joints as I rout the sockets for the case dividers.

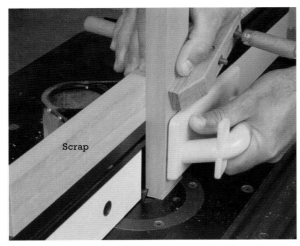

Two passes across the router table creates the dovetail on the end of the divider. The scrap above stabilizes the workpiece.

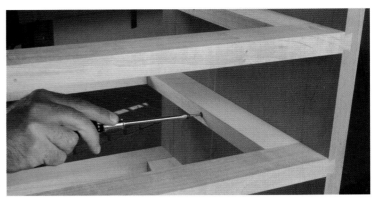

A screw driven into the case side helps keep it flat throughout the years.

templates ready next time I receive an order for the chest. You may prefer to use one template; start with the uppermost set of dividers and reduce the length of the template after each set of cuts.

After cutting the sockets, I'll rout the dovetails on the ends of the dividers with the same 14° dovetail bit in my router table. But first I cut the dividers to the final length, which corresponds to the distance between the sockets. Instead of measuring, I position the end of the divider in one socket and mark the length at the opposite socket. This method eliminates potential measuring errors.

All of the dividers should be the same length. I mark the divider closest to the top of the case, clamp a stop on the saw and cut all dividers to this length. You may find that the sides of the case have bowed slightly; the dividers will push or pull the bow out of the case as they're installed. In contrast, if you cut each divider a different length to correspond with the bow, the case will remain permanently bowed.

Next, I mount the dovetail bit in my router table and run the stock through twice to cut the tail, one pass on each face. The end of the divider has a small footprint; in fact, it's too small to steady the workpiece as you push it across the router table. For additional support I clamp a stick of wood to the divider at a right angle. The stick rides along the top of the fence to support the divider while making the cut. I use a push block to keep the workpiece firmly against the

fence and distance my hand from the router bit.

Before cutting the dovetails on the dividers I first test the fit on a sample piece of stock. The dovetail should fit snug within the socket and require gentle taps with a mallet to coax it together. Unlike a row of dovetails on a box, this joint doesn't have mating long-grain surfaces for glue; for the joint to be strong the fit must be somewhat tight. Before you go to the next step remember to cut and dovetail the short center divider at the top drawer opening.

Runners

With the dovetails cut on the dividers, you're ready to work on the runners. Besides supporting a drawer, each pair of runners also serves as a kicker to keep the drawer below from tipping as it is opened. The runners have 1"-long tenons on each end that fit in mortises in the dividers. After assembly each runner is fastened to the case side with one or two screws. Once screwed to the case side, the runner serves as a batten to prevent the case side from warping. Stagger the locations of the screws, so they're not in a straight line. Here's where you can run into a cross-grain construction problem.

As the case sides contract during the dry, winter months the runners can push the dovetailed dividers out of the case. Cut the runners ⅛" short to leave room for seasonal movement. During assembly, apply glue only at the mortise-and-tenon joint at the front. The tenon at the

back is dry and has a ⅛" gap at the shoulder. As the sides contract, the rear tenon will slide into the mortise. When the relative humidity rises during the summer months, the case sides will expand and the tenons will slide out slightly.

Once the joints are cut, you're ready to apply glue, and assemble the dividers and runners within the case. Begin by gluing the front dividers in place. Use caution and apply pressure equally to each end of the divider as you fit it into the case; if the divider is installed askew it will bind and may break the joint. Next, glue the runners into the front dividers. The last step is to glue in the back dividers. Remember, the back dividers are glued to the case but not to the runners. Once all the parts are in place the case is amazingly rigid.

Feet

With the "box" completed, turn your attention to the feet. Besides supporting the case, the feet and crown moulding transform the box into a piece of furniture. Miters join the feet at the front; half-blind dovetails join the feet at the rear to the poplar support blocks, cut from one 12"-long board. Once the joints are cut and fit, I band saw the foot's profile. Then I assemble the feet; first the dovetails, then the miters. To glue the miters apply a coat of yellow glue to each half of the miter, rub the joint together, check for square, and let it sit while the glue dries; no clamping is necessary. After the glue has dried reinforce the miter with a glue block in the back. The grain in the glue block must run horizontally to correspond with the grain in the foot. Otherwise the foot may crack with seasonal humidity changes.

A standard-angle block plane with a 55° cutting angle is useful for leveling the joints. This high cutting angle reduces tearout in some tricky woods.

Note that the grain pattern in the glue block is parallel to the grain pattern of the foot to which it's applied.

Apply a liberal coat of glue to the miter for the moulding. The glue ensures the miter will stay tight over time.

Align the two halves of the miter and hold the joint in position for a minute or two.

The base frame is glued at the front only, and the front edge is glued under the bottom edge of the case bottom. The rest of the frame is attached with screws in slots. Glue blocks, ½" square, connect the feet to the frame.

Crown Moulding

The crown moulding is shaped from solid stock by using a series of passes over a router table. It's not possible to use flat architectural-style crown moulding because it creates a void on the top of the case. Instead, it's necessary to use triangular stock. To avoid excessive waste I band saw a rectangular plank diagonally as shown in the illustration on page 61.

After shaping the moulding, I carefully miter the front piece; the length of the front strip of moulding is critical. If it's too long it will prevent the returns from coming in full contact with the case and create a gap. If it's too short, it creates a gap in the miter. I miter the first end of the moulding, mark the opposite end

and "creep" up to the miter with the saw. Once I'm satisfied with the front strip of crown moulding, I miter the "returns" or side pieces to match. Then I cut the other end of the returns flush with the back of the case.

The next step is to attach the crown moulding to the case. I attach the front strip of crown moulding with glue. Because the grain direction on the case corresponds with that on the moulding, glue will hold the piece secure without interfering with seasonal wood movement. However, the return mouldings must be attached to allow for seasonal movement in the case side. Otherwise, the case sides will crack. To solve the problem, I apply glue to the miter as well as the first couple inches of the moulding. I attach the remainder of the moulding with a couple screws from inside the case. In order to allow the case sides to expand without restriction from the moulding, I slot the screw holes in the case sides.

Back

I use ½"-thick poplar for the backboards. The edges of the boards are shiplapped. I wait to attach them to the case once the finishing is complete. This provides easy access to the inside of the case for finishing.

Specialty Lumber Dealers

Good Hope Hardwoods
610-255-5245 or
goodhope.com

Groff & Groff
800-342-0001 or
groffslumber.com

Hearne Hardwoods
888-814-0007 or
hearnehardwoods.com

Irion Lumber
570-724-1895 or
irionlumber.com

Solid Carcase Joinery: Half-blind Dovetails

1 — Begin by marking the baseline on the ends of the sides.

2 — Mark the baseline on the faces of the top (left) and bottom (right).

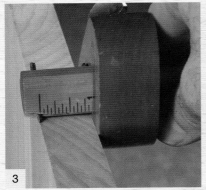

3 — Set the gauge to equal the thickness of the top and bottom.

4 — Mark the inside face of the sides.

5 — Begin by marking the half-tail, which covers the back rabbet.

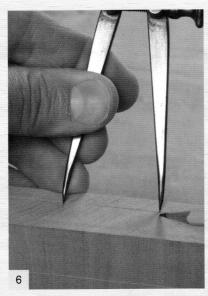

6 — Use dividers to accurately step off the location of each pin.

7 — Mark the slope of each pin.

8 — Transfer the pin layout to the mating board.

9 — Use a square to mark the sides of the pins.

10 — The pin board layout is complete.

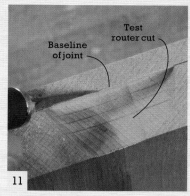

11

Set the depth of the router bit so that it slightly contacts the baseline.

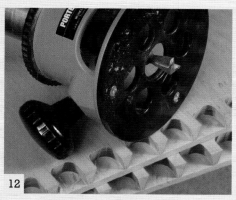

12

As you rout the space between the pins, avoid undercutting the back wall, which can weaken the joint.

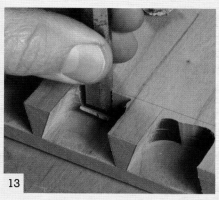

13

Finish each space by chopping out the corners with a sharp chisel.

14

The pins are complete and ready for marking the corresponding tails.

15

Position the pin board over the tail board and mark the tails with a knife.

16

Transfer the marks to the end with a square.

17

Saw each tail to the baseline.

18

Chisel the space between each tail.

19

Tap the joint together with a mallet.

The Art of Making Dovetailed Drawers

BY MARIO RODRIGUEZ

There are just a few things my partner at Philadelphia Furniture Workshops, Alan Turner, and I don't see eye-to-eye on. But how to make a good drawer isn't one of them. When building furniture, we probably spend as much time making the drawers as we do making the piece itself. But this is an aspect of furniture-making many woodworkers don't devote enough attention to. In this chapter, I'll explain and illustrate how I built a pair of drawers for a small writing desk.

Drawers bestow even the finest handcrafted furniture with a utilitarian character by arranging, storing and providing access to objects. Yet it's important that their number, size and placement contribute to the purpose and appearance of a piece, not detract from it.

Drawers are expected to operate easily, without sticking or rattling around. Drawer bottoms shouldn't sag or be left rough-sawn, and joints shouldn't be sloppy. Drawers shouldn't be an afterthought, disappointing the viewer and diminishing the experience.

When open, a drawer should reveal craftsmanship and quality consistent with the rest of the piece. You wouldn't go to the trouble of reproducing a Philadelphia highboy, then fit its drawers with metal slides.

Features of a First-class Drawer

No matter what type of drawers you build, there are several essentials to good drawer making:

- Good design. Drawers should be consistent with the piece being built.
- Good material. Use the best that can be obtained; whether it's solid or plywood.
- Careful measurements. Your measurements must be exact; measure carefully, then double-check the figures.
- Good, sound techniques. Basic skills on machines and with hand tools will produce crisp, clean work.
- Patience. Take it easy; making and fitting a drawer will take time and may test your patience.

These drawers are supported by and ride upon a web frame consisting of two latitudinal rails (front and rear) and three longitudinal rails (two side, one center).

Details make the difference. The drawers ride on the rails of the web frame, and the guides restrain movement from side to side.

Drawer guides were attached to the web to track the drawers into the openings at the front of the desk. When initially installed, each guide intrudes slightly into the drawer opening by $\frac{1}{16}$". Later, the guides are carefully planed to allow the drawers easy and smooth travel.

The height of this desk is 29" below the top. I allowed 24½" leg clearance, giving me 4½" for top and bottom rails, and my drawers. The combined thickness of the rails is 1½", so I had 3" for the drawers. That is a good height for most objects stored in a typical desk. These drawers will be almost 14" wide and 18" deep, which is also a good size. A drawer that is deeper than it is wide will operate easily without racking or sticking.

Selecting Material

For the drawer fronts select clean, well-behaved material – something mild and easy to plane. For this desk, I selected a single piece of mahogany, long enough for both drawer fronts and the center dividing strip between the drawers, then milled it to ¾" thickness.

For the drawer sides carefully choose your stock. Quartersawn stock is ideal; it's stable, won't twist or warp, and is easy to plane. I carefully went through a stack of maple boards, and selected the ones with the cleanest, straightest grain. Maple is a tight-grained hard-wearing wood, ideal for drawer sides. Mahogany or oak are other good choices.

Many woodworkers make the mistake

If you resaw thicker boards for drawer material, sticker them and let them sit for several days to acclimate before milling the stock to final dimensions.

of using material that is too thick, which produces heavy, clunky drawers. This is a small desk and the drawers will hold small, lightweight objects and supplies, so milling the sides to thin dimensions maintained the delicate nature and scale of the piece. You should proportion your drawer stock to the piece. For instance, drawer stock for an 18th-century spice box or a contemporary jewelry box might be as thin as ⅛".

Hardwood isn't usually commercially available in less than 1" thickness, so I resaw my stock. This often means interior surfaces of the wood with different moisture content than the exterior will be exposed, which can cause some move-

Fitting the width of the drawer side to the height of the opening before building the drawer gives more control of the process.

ment. If you resaw, anticipate some slight twisting or cupping, so mill extra stock and select the best for your drawers.

Milling & Joining the Parts

After a preliminary milling, sticker the stock while you work on the rest of the project to help it acclimate to the shop environment. Then, as you approach your drawer-making, take the boards down to their finished thickness.

Rip the sides ⅟₃₂" narrower than the opening and leave them about 1" longer than necessary in case you need to re-cut the dovetails. And, if possible, orient the grain direction to make it easier to plane and fit the completed drawer later.

Drawer fronts should be ripped and cut to fit precisely into their openings, with barely a hairline gap all around. You should try for a tight, close fit at this stage. When fitting the completed drawer boxes, the drawer front can always be planed to achieve the desired fit and appearance.

Dovetails are regarded as the strongest and most attractive way to join two perpendicular pieces of wood with the grain running the same direction. I like to use half-blind dovetails to join the drawer sides to the fronts and through-dovetails for the side-to-back joints. They have a distinctive and attractive appearance. They also provide the added benefit of squaring the drawer during glue-up, often eliminating the need for clamps.

To lay out your dovetails, follow the

1:8 rule or just lay them out at 10°, with half tails at each end and two full tails centered on the remaining space. I first make a sheet-metal template that gives me a clear pattern (that can be reused) to mark onto the drawer sides.

After marking the tails on the drawer sides, scribe the dovetail baseline onto the ends of the drawer front about ¼" from the face. This amount makes for a good appearance and a strong joint. On the interior surface of the drawer front, scribe a line about ⅟₃₂" less than the thickness of the drawer side. That way, when the drawer box is assembled, the drawer side will sit proud of the drawer front, which allows the side to be planed flush with the end of the drawer face, without altering the size of the carefully fitted drawer front. This also makes glue-up easier because you won't have to worry about damaging the delicate pins.

When cutting your tails first, you can cut directly to the line, remove the waste at the baseline and not fiddle with lots of tedious clean up. If the saw drifts a little, that's OK – as long as the kerf is narrow, clean and straight. Any deviation from the scribed outline can be transferred over to the pin board. Remember: Half-blind dovetails are only seen from one side, so the parts can be undercut and relieved to ease the fit without compromising the appearance or strength of the joint.

Next, carefully mark the outline of the tails onto the pin board (drawer front).

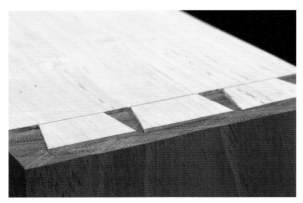

Cutting the dovetails to leave the sides extended from the drawer front simplifies fitting and maintains the smallest possible gap between the drawer and carcase.

With thin drawer stock a jeweler's saw or coping saw will remove the waste between tails quickly and without the risk of damaging the work by chopping between the tails with a chisel.

Cut the pins fat and pare them just shy of the line. The wide spaces between the pins will provide easy access from two angles. A partial test fit will reveal any excess material that has to be removed. I always say that folks won't notice a small discrepancy in spacing or angle in your dovetails – they'll only notice the gaps!

After fitting the drawer fronts to the sides and checking the dovetails for fit and appearance, cut a groove between the pins along the inside of the drawer fronts to accept the drawer bottoms. The placement of this groove is important for two reasons. First, it should be hidden when the drawer is assembled. Second, it should be situated to maximize your storage space.

Thin Sides Call for Slips

If you mill your sides to a thin dimension, you should consider using drawer slips for reinforcement and extra strength. Thin drawer sides might not be thick enough to support the drawer bottom, which is commonly held in place with a groove cut into the sides.

Drawer slips are small mouldings, placed along the interior of the drawer sides to prevent their splitting under a load or heavy use. They also add character and detail.

I cut the slips on the table saw with a careful sequence of cuts that yielded the slender parts. I milled them to a profile that was adequate to support the drawer bottom, yet would only minimally intrude upon the usable space of the drawer.

The sides and back of the drawer are joined with through-dovetails. These can be a little tricky because thin stock will dictate small dovetails. And if the stock is very thin, it can split when you cut the joint. However, one small advantage is they won't be seen unless the drawer is fully withdrawn.

Before laying out the joint, measure the location of the drawer-bottom groove (from the drawer front) and cut enough material off the drawer back to allow the drawer bottom to be slipped underneath it when the drawers are assembled. Don't forget to cut off the excess length of the drawer sides. My sides-to-front dovetails turned out good enough that I didn't need a second chance at them.

The slot for the drawer bottom is located in the space for the lowest tail in the drawer front.

The angled top of the slip bridges the corner between the sides of the drawer and the bottom.

Glued in place, the slip strengthens the lower portion of the drawer bottom. The back of the drawer is narrower than the side so that the drawer bottom can be slid into place after finishing.

After cutting the through-dovetails for the side-to-back joints, dry-fitting the drawer boxes, checking dimensions and sanding the parts, I glued them up. If the dovetails are well executed, the drawers should come together without clamps. However, if you do need clamps, check the drawers for square. You should also check for flat by placing them on a flat surface. A twisted drawer will severely complicate the installation later.

When gluing up, keep a damp rag nearby. It's a lot easier to remove excess glue from the inside of the drawer at glue-up than to allow it to dry and have to chisel it out later.

When the glue in the drawer boxes is dry, measure and cut the drawer slips to fit against the inside of the drawer front and back. Then align the slips with the groove on the drawer front and the bottom of the drawer back; glue and clamp them in place.

When appropriate, use solid wood for the bottoms. For this desk, I cut a couple of ⁵⁄₁₆"-thickness leaves from a 1"-thick piece and bookmatched them. After gluing up the panels, sand them to fair the seam and smooth the surface.

Taking the bottoms down to ⁵⁄₁₆" kept them thick enough while making them lightweight, too. After cutting them to size, I rabbeted three edges. By rabbeting the edges I could slip them into a ³⁄₁₆" groove, yet maintain their ⁵⁄₁₆" thickness.

Because the drawers were narrow, I oriented the grain front-to-back, because I wasn't concerned with any significant wood movement. This means that grain shrinkage or swelling will take place across the drawer. When making your drawer bottoms and orienting the grain, take the size of the drawer into account. Generally, you want to run the grain in the direction of the longest dimension. So, a drawer that measures 16" deep and 24" wide would have the grain running side to side.

Fits Like a Glove

On a cabinet, I would remove the back before fitting the drawers. This provides easier access and the opportunity to "eyeball" any problems not visible from the outside. In this case, I left the top off the desk.

When the drawers are ready, plane the sides flush with the front; be careful not to reduce the size of the drawer front. I plane a little more off the back end of a drawer, making the back slightly narrower than the front. This allows the drawer to initially enter the cavity with ease and tighten up slightly as it hits home.

I attempted to slide the drawer into its recess. But it was still too large to clear the opening. A few careful passes with a plane over the drawer sides fixed that. However, the box still wouldn't slide fully into the desk. With a sharp block plane, I took light shavings from the drawer guides (which were glued to the drawer web and flanked the opening) on each side. The guides are rabbeted and stop 2" short of the back apron, so their full length can be easily trimmed with a block plane. With several light, careful strokes, the drawers were planed to a tight fit.

Now the opening can be adjusted more precisely. By carefully planing the sides of the drawers I was able to achieve a tight 1/32" gap all around the drawer front. But with the drawer resting on the frame, there was no reveal/gap along the bottom. This is one of the last steps in fitting a drawer and should be performed in a slow and careful manner.

To create an even gap, I scribe a line with a marking gauge and, using a tiny rabbet plane, I cut a small rabbet along the bottom edge of the drawer front. On a larger drawer, I'd use my shoulder plane.

Once the drawers are fitted, you can apply a small amount of wax to the bottom edges of the drawer sides and the guides. When you're satisfied with the operation of the drawers and their alignment with and to the front of the desk, you can set the drawer stops in place. These are three small blocks that are glued and clamped onto the front rail of the drawer web, just behind the drawer fronts.

Some woodworkers choose to leave the drawer interiors unfinished; others finish them exactly as the rest of the piece. It's a good idea to provide some form of protection. I recommend a light coat of shellac, lacquer or just wax. I finished these drawers with a very light coat of sprayed-on satin lacquer, rubbed out and waxed.

The rabbet in the drawer bottom matches the width of the grooves in the drawer sides and front. The extra thickness in the bottom keeps it from sagging.

The drawer guides have a rabbet on the bottom and stop short of the back. This allows them to be planed during the fitting process.

A small rabbet on the underside of the drawer front provides an even reveal to match the gaps at the top and sides.

Assembling and fitting the drawer before installing the drawer bottom allows precise placement of stops glued to the lower rail.

Build a Better Cabinet

BY CHRISTOPHER SCHWARZ

Woodworking magazines and books are cluttered with explanations of how to do the small stuff: cut an accurate joint, prepare a surface for finishing or build a door or drawer. What is mostly absent is a discussion of how to put those small steps together into a system of building that makes sense.

I've been in shops all over the world, and each has a different way of gluing boards together to make cabinets, doors and tables. All of the systems work. But some waste time. Some require precise measuring. And some curry simple, obvious and disastrous errors – such as making a door that is 1" too small.

About 10 years ago, I started spending time with Troy Sexton, a cabinetmaker in Sunbury, Ohio, who builds early American pieces in his one-person shop. Troy is unusual in that he has spent lots of time compressing the procedures to make a cabinet so that he reduces error at every turn, and he arranges each step in building a cabinet so the process flows smoothly.

Many people would say that Troy builds cabinets backward. He starts with the face frame, then he builds the doors and hangs them in the face frame. Then he builds the carcase and fits the drawers. In other shops, they typically start with building the carcase of the project, then they build the face frame and attach it to the carcase. Then they hang the doors in the openings and finally build the drawers to suit.

After adopting Troy's "face frame first" method years ago, I found other professional woodworkers who also work that way, and I started tweaking this method to incorporate handplanes into the system (Troy uses power equipment almost exclusively). What follows is the result of lots of trials, errors and cabinets.

Why Build the Face Frame First?

Not every cabinet uses a face frame. If you live on the West Coast or prefer modern furniture, chances are you aren't going to attach a face frame to your cabinet. If you build these so-called "frame-less" cabinets, move on to the next section.

But if you build American furniture in historical styles from the 17th to mid-

If you build the face frame of a cabinet first, you can save construction time and reduce mistakes caused by measuring. Plus, this technique works well in a shop that uses both hand and power tools.

20th centuries, chances are that your cabinets will have a face frame – a framework of ¾"-thick wood that defines the openings of your doors and drawers and strengthens the carcase behind it.

Building the face frame first has several advantages. First, it uses less material than any other step in the process. So if you make a serious goof, you're not out a lot of material.

Second: The face frame determines the size of your doors and drawers. So once those are fixed by the construction of the frame, you can then build your doors with confidence.

Third, you can hang the doors in the face frame more easily with the face frame detached from the carcase. Most woodworkers hang their doors after the face frame is on the carcase. So they are fighting gravity all the way home. Either the cabinet is upright and they are balancing the door on its skinny bottom edge, or the cabinet is on its back and the door is prone to droop into the carcase. This is a problem particularly if the doors are inset into the frame instead of doors with edges that lip over the face frame.

It's far easier to fit a door when everything is flat on your workbench or

The 'Face Frame First' Approach to Cabinets

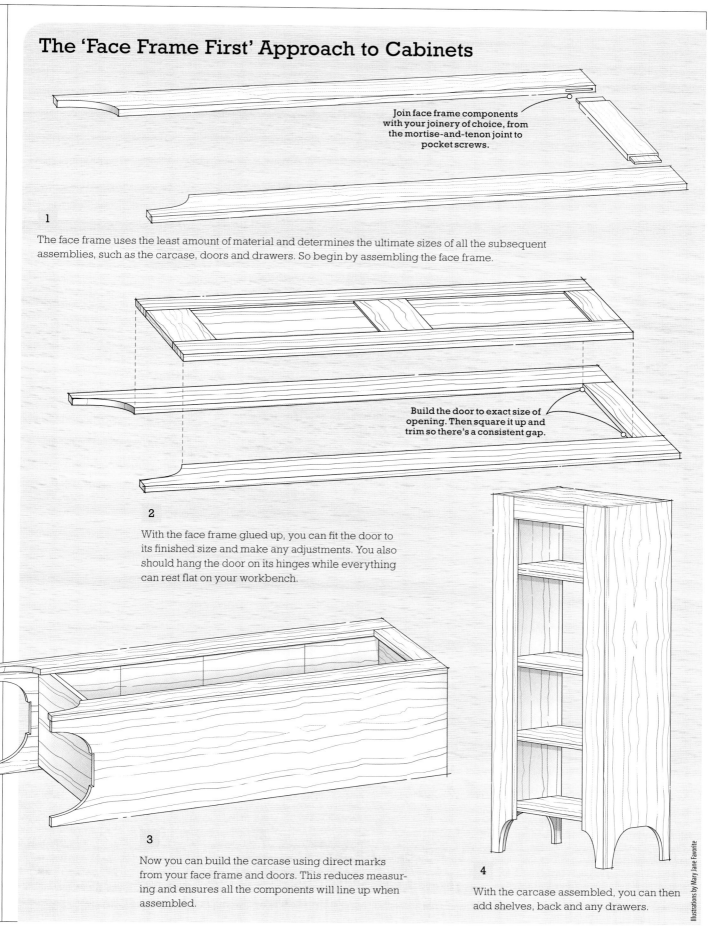

Join face frame components with your joinery of choice, from the mortise-and-tenon joint to pocket screws.

1

The face frame uses the least amount of material and determines the ultimate sizes of all the subsequent assemblies, such as the carcase, doors and drawers. So begin by assembling the face frame.

Build the door to exact size of opening. Then square it up and trim so there's a consistent gap.

2

With the face frame glued up, you can fit the door to its finished size and make any adjustments. You also should hang the door on its hinges while everything can rest flat on your workbench.

3

Now you can build the carcase using direct marks from your face frame and doors. This reduces measuring and ensures all the components will line up when assembled.

4

With the carcase assembled, you can then add shelves, back and any drawers.

Illustrations by Mary Jane Favorite

assembly table. Plus you have easy access to both the inside and outside of the face frame – something you give up when you attach the face frame to the carcase.

Also, you do less measuring. You can use your assembled face frame and door to directly lay out the dados in your carcase sides. So there's less opportunity for a measurement error.

And finally, building the face frame first allows you to make mistakes from which you can easily recover. Say you place a rail at the wrong position when you build your face frame. No problem.

You simply adjust the size of your doors and change the position of your shelves and dividers to suit. If you build the carcase first, a mistake on the face frame usually means that the face frame is headed for the scrap pile.

The Frameless Variant

If your cabinet is a frameless one, you should begin with building the doors. The doors will then determine where the dividers will go in the carcase. Once you build your doors, you can lay them directly on your case sides to mark out

where the dados should go for shelves and dividers – this also reduces errors.

Incorporating Handplanes

The face-frame first system works great with power tools, but many beginning hand-tool users might be confused about how to incorporate planes into the system. Here's how:

Most woodworkers know that the jointer plane is for flattening stock and the smoothing plane is for preparing it for finishing, but some get confused as to when these planes should be used in construction. Is the jointer plane used before or after assembly? Do you smooth plane the finished assemblies or the individual pieces?

Part of the answer is contained in the names of the planes. The jointer plane flattens the stock before the joinery. The smoothing plane is used when assembly is complete and you get to a point where the next step won't allow you to use a plane. For example, you should smooth plane the side of a carcase right before you attach the moulding. After you attach the moulding the smoothing plane can't access that entire area.

So let's walk through the three types of assemblies in furniture construction: frames, slab boxes and tables/stools to see how planes can be incorporated into the "face frame first" approach.

Frames: Face Frames & Doors

After preparing all the stock with my power jointer and planer for my face frame, I'll flatten all the boards with a jointer plane before cutting the joinery on them. The jointer plane removes the milling marks, twists, cups and bows left over from the power equipment.

Then cut your joints and plane the rails only with either a smoothing plane or a jointer plane set up for a fine cut. This will make the horizontal rails a bit thinner than their adjoining vertical stiles. If there's a panel that goes into this frame, flatten it with a jointer plane, cut the joinery on it and smooth plane it before assembly.

Then assemble the frame. When the glue is dry you have a frame where the rails and panel are ready for finish, but the long stiles are slightly proud. So use

Here I'm thinning down the rails a bit more than the stiles with a jointer plane that is set up like a smoothing plane. Then I'll assemble this frame and smooth plane the long stiles to finished thickness.

If you look closely at this photo you can see the stiles are slightly proud of the rails. Thinning the stiles is easier than thinning the rails with a handplane because most face frames are vertical and so they fit on your benchtop better that way.

With the face frame and door flat on my work surface, it's much easier to position the door so there is a uniform gap all around. Plus adding the hinges is a great deal easier.

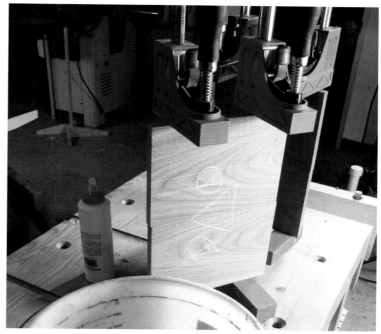

The individual boards in these panels have been prepped with a jointer plane. Then I glued up the panels and will be able to go right to the smoothing plane because the seams are tidy and flush.

a smoothing plane to reduce the stiles in thickness to the same thickness as the rails. This takes some practice to do well, but you'll be an expert after a couple attempts.

Then build the doors, fit them and hang the doors on their hinges.

Dealing with Panels & Boxes

Most solid-wood carcases involve some sort of slab sides or slab shelves. As a result, you need to glue up several boards into wider panels. Here's how you do that with handplanes: First arrange the individual boards for best appearance when you plan your panel, but try to get the grain running in all the same direction in the slab. This makes it easier to plane after assembly.

Then use the jointer plane on all your individual boards to flatten them. Now you can cut any joinery on the boards' long edges. Some woodworkers use splines, some use biscuits, many use nothing but the glue. When you glue things up, make every effort to keep the boards flush at the seams. If you struggle with this step, switch to a slow-setting glue, such as liquid hide glue.

When the glue has cured, remove the

panel from the clamps and evaluate it. If you kept your seams flush, you should be able to clean up the panel with a smoothing plane to remove glue and dress the panel to go in a frame.

If you have misalignments at the seams (more than 1/32"), you need to attack the panel with a jointer plane – first diagonally to the grain and then with it. This gets the panel back to a flat state in an efficient manner (a jointer plane takes a cut that is about three or four times thicker than that of a smoothing plane).

With the panel flat and the glue removed, you can cut the joinery on it. Cut your dados, grooves and rabbets. Then assemble the carcase with your flattened slabs. Or if you are making a raised panel for a frame, cut its moulded edge, and then prepare it for finishing with a smoothing plane.

With the carcase assembled, you can then attach the face frame (if you have one) and then smooth plane the entire carcase for finishing.

Tables, Stools, Post-and-rail

The other kind of assembly is similar to a stool or table. You have stretchers or aprons running between thick legs or

posts. These are treated much like a frame construction with a minor variation. Use the jointer plane to dress all the surfaces, then cut your joinery. Then smooth plane everything before assembly.

The reason you do this is that the legs will likely be too fragile to smooth plane after assembly. After assembly, you might have to clean up some spots with a plane, scraper or sandpaper, but you want to minimize this because the assembly is awkward to secure to your workbench.

After assembly, you will need to level the top edges of the aprons so they're level to the top of the legs. Do this with a jointer plane. Then you can go on to build your table or stool's top using the procedures above for slab panels.

The techniques above don't account for every single situation in the shop, but the principles are sound. Use your jointer plane to get your stock flat at the first. Assemble your cabinets by first tackling the assembly that uses the least amount of wood and is the most critical. And keep your mind open for new ways to work.

Pleasant Hill Firewood Box

BY CHRISTOPHER SCHWARZ

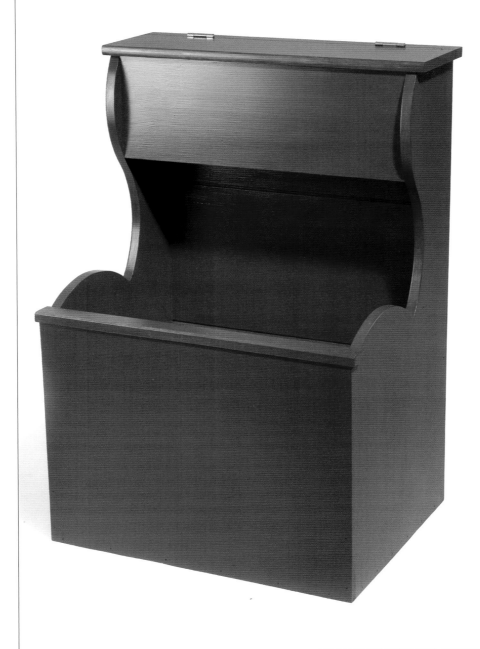

The buildings at the Shaker Village in Pleasant Hill, Ky., are filled with handy firewood boxes. After a few visits to the colony, I concluded that this example is the best one.

Tucked into a room in the Centre Family Dwelling, this firewood box represents what I like about the Western Shaker furniture styles. This box has a few graceful and unexpected curves, yet it still looks decidedly Shaker.

Building this box is simple. With the exception of the curves on the sides, all the cuts are straight. With the exception of the hinged lid, all the joinery on the box is glue and nails.

The biggest construction challenge is gluing up narrower boards into the panels that make up the box's sides, front and bottom. I glued these up using pocket screws as clamps.

However, because this project is painted, there's an easier solution at the home center. In the lumber section of the store you'll likely find wide laminated pine panels that are pieced together at a factory from narrow strips. If you purchase this material, you won't have to glue up any panels and can go right to cutting.

The other option is to buy No. 2 common 1 x 12s. I bought five 8'-long 1 x 12s so I could cut around knots. I also bought a small piece of ¼"-thick Masonite. Why? Read on.

Make a Template

When you're working out a complex design or need to make multiple and identical parts, a full-size template is handy.

With this project, a full-size template helps you get the curves just right and helps you fit the pieces to the hinged kindling box. Plus, if you ever need to make more of these boxes, the template will give you a good head start.

Use the illustration to draw your template on the Masonite using a ruler and a compass. All the curves are a 7" radius, so the layout work is easy. Cut the template to shape using a jigsaw and sand the edges until the template looks good and has smooth edges. If you want to adjust the design, here's your chance to alter it and see how it looks. Glue up all the panels you need and get ready to cut the sides.

Construction

Trace the template's shape on your side pieces and cut them with your jigsaw. Clamp the two sides together and shape the curves with a rasp and sandpaper so the two are identical. Using the side pieces as a guide, determine the actual width of the box's bottom, the width of the bottom of the kindling box and the width of the front of the kindling box. Cut these three pieces to finished size. Glue and nail them between the sides.

Now work on the front of the box. Cut this panel as close to size as possible – I like to leave it a hair long. Glue and nail the front to the carcase. Trim any overhang with your block plane or #100-grit sandpaper.

Now repeat the same process with the back pieces. I used three horizontal boards for the back. Two of the boards were 1 x 12s. The third one was ripped to fit just right. If you like, you can plane a small chamfer on the back boards' long edges as a decorative detail. This adds a shadow line where the backboards meet one another.

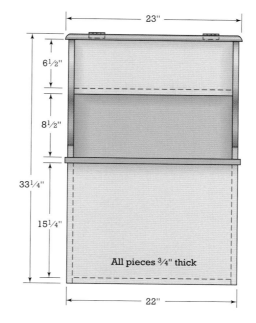

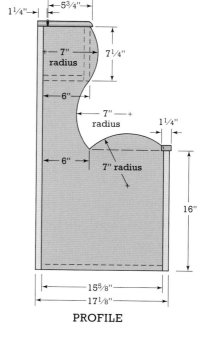

ELEVATION

PROFILE

Crosscut the hinge rail and lid at the same time so they are the same length. Your miter saw is an excellent tool for this sort of operation. Screw your hinges to both the hinge rail and the lid. Then glue and nail the hinge rail to the carcase.

The last bit of construction is the box's front edge. I took the difficult route to fit this piece in place. I notched out the underside of the workpiece with a hand-saw and chisel so the notches nest neatly over the curve on the sides. You can fit the piece any way your skills or tools allow.

Disassemble the lid and hinges and sand the project up to #150-grit. Break all the sharp edges of the piece by hand with a piece of old sandpaper. The finish is simply three coats of semi-gloss paint. As shown, this piece is a little more barn

red than the original. But it is still a red that is consistent with the original Shaker paint recipes. You should, of course, finish yours to suit your decor.

Watch those curves. A full-size template helps in many ways. It allows you to refine the design details, determine the finished sizes of key components and to lay out your cuts.

Firewood Box

NO.	ITEM	DIMENSIONS (INCHES)			MATERIAL	COMMENTS
		T	W	L		
2	Sides	3/4	15 5/8	32 1/2	Pine	
1	Front	3/4	16	22	Pine	
	Back	3/4	32 1/2	22	Pine	Three boards
1	Bottom	3/4	15 5/8	20 1/2	Pine	
1	Kindling box bottom	3/4	5 1/4	20 1/2	Pine	
1	Kindling box front	3/4	7 1/4	20 1/2	Pine	
1	Kindling box lid	3/4	5 3/4	23	Pine	
1	Hinge rail	3/4	1 1/4	23	Pine	
1	Front edge	3/4	1 1/4	22 1/2	Pine	Notched around sides

Your First Cabinet

BY TROY SEXTON

I've built hundreds of single-door cabinets like this one. Some people use them as spice cabinets. Others use them in the bathroom as a medicine cabinet.

As I was building this particular cabinet, it occurred to me that it would be an excellent project for beginners. It has all the traditional components of larger-scale cabinetry, yet it doesn't need a lot of material or tooling. Once you've built this cabinet, you can build something bigger using the same principles. Intermediate woodworkers might also pick up a trick or two because I build my cabinets just a bit differently.

Choose Your Wood

I used tiger maple for this project, but if this is your first cabinet, you might want to use poplar and then paint the finished item. Poplar is easy to work with and less expensive than maple, especially if the maple has some figure.

As in larger cabinets, most of the major components are made from ¾"-thick stock: the case sides, top, bottom, plus the rails and stiles for the door and the face frame. This cabinet has a solid wood shiplapped back that's made from ½"-thick pieces; the door panel is ⅝" thick.

Face Frame: the Place to Start

It seems logical to begin by constructing the case. Don't. The size of your case and door are all determined by your face frame. Build it first and then you'll use your face frame to lay out your case and door. All face frames are made up of rails and stiles, much like a door. The stiles are the vertical pieces. The rails are the horizontal pieces that go between the stiles.

When you rip your stiles to width on your table saw, make the rip ¹⁄₁₆" wider than stated on the cutting list. You need this extra to overhang the sides of your case so you can trim it flush with a flush-cutting bit in a router. Once your pieces are cut to size, join the rails and stiles using mortise-and-tenon joints.

Begin by cutting the tenons on the rail ends. I know the books say to cut the mortise first, but I've found it's easier to lay out your mortises after your tenons are cut. Try it, and I think you'll agree.

The tenons should be ⅜" thick (one-half as thick as your stock), centered on the rail and 1" long. I cut ½" shoulders on the tenons. If they're any smaller, the mortise might blow out. Now use your tenons to lay out your mortises on the stiles. Hold the tenon flat against the edge where the mortise will go and use the tenon like a ruler to mark your mortise.

Now cut your mortises. Make them all 1¹⁄₁₆" deep, which will prevent your 1"-long tenons from bottoming out. You don't want your tenons to wobble in your mortises, yet you don't want to have to beat the tenon in place.

Dry-fit your face frame, then put glue on the mortise walls and clamp it up. While you're waiting for it to dry, turn your attention to the bead moulding that goes on the inside edge of the face frames.

Years ago, I used to cut the beading into the rails and stiles. Then I would have to miter the bead and cut away the beading where the rails and stiles were joined. It sounds like a pain, and it was. Now I simply make my bead moulding separate from my face frame and miter, nail and glue it in place. It looks just as good.

To make the bead moulding, put a ¼"

beading bit in your router and mount it in a router table. Then take a ¾"-thick board that's about 4" wide and cut the bead on one edge. Take that board to your table saw, set your rip fence to make a ⅜"-wide cut and rip the bead from the wide board. Repeat this process three more times.

Now take your strips and run them through your planer to reduce them in

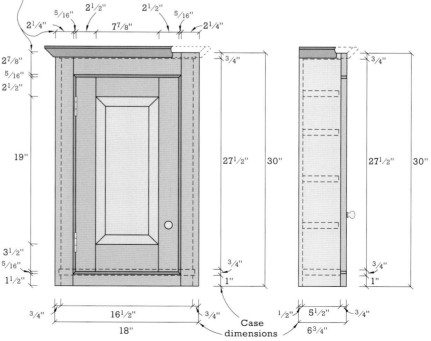

Face frame/door dimensions

Case dimensions

Adding this beaded moulding to the inside of the face frame creates a nice shadow line around the door. Miter, glue and nail it in place. Don't forget to putty your nail holes.

Fit your door in the face frame before you attach the face frame to the case. Everything lays flat on your bench as you work. You'll find this procedure is a faster and easier way to get perfect results.

thickness to $\frac{5}{16}$". Miter the corners; then glue and nail them in place. Sand both sides of your face frame with #100-grit sandpaper and move on to building the door.

The Door

Why make the door next? Well, for one thing, it is easier to hang your door in your face frame before you nail the face frame to your case.

I build my doors so they are the same size as my opening, then I shave off a little so there's a $\frac{1}{16}$" gap all around. This way if the door or face frame is out of square, I can taper the door edges to fit, hiding my error.

The door is built much like the face frame, using the same size mortises and tenons. The biggest difference is that you will need to cut a groove in your rails and stiles for the door panel, so your tenons must be haunched. A "haunch" is a little extra width in the tenon's shoulder that fills in the groove on the end of the stile.

Begin by cutting a $\frac{3}{8}$"-deep x $\frac{3}{8}$"-wide groove down the center of one long edge of your rails and stiles. Cut your tenons

on your rails. Then cut your mortises on your stiles. Dry fit the pieces together and measure how big the center panel should be.

You want the panel to float to allow seasonal expansion and contraction, so cut the panel to allow $\frac{1}{8}$" expansion on either side. Now raise the door panel using your table saw or a cutter in your router table. Practice on scrap pieces of $\frac{5}{8}$" stock so you achieve the right lip, angle and fit.

When the panel is complete, sand the raised section, then glue up the door. Be

Spice Cabinet

NO.	ITEM	DIMENSIONS (INCHES)		
		T	W	L
2	Face frame stiles	$\frac{3}{4}$	$2\frac{1}{4}$	30
1	Top face frame rail	$\frac{3}{4}$	$2\frac{7}{8}$	$15\frac{1}{2}$
1	Bot face frame rail	$\frac{3}{4}$	$1\frac{1}{2}$	$15\frac{1}{2}$
2	Door stiles	$\frac{3}{4}$	$2\frac{1}{2}$	25
1	Top door rail	$\frac{3}{4}$	$2\frac{1}{2}$	$9\frac{7}{8}$
1	Bot door rail	$\frac{3}{4}$	$3\frac{1}{2}$	$9\frac{7}{8}$
1	Door panel	$\frac{5}{8}$	$8\frac{3}{8}$	$19\frac{1}{2}$
2	Case sides	$\frac{3}{4}$	6	30
2	Top & Bot	$\frac{3}{4}$	$5\frac{1}{2}$	17
4	Shelves	$\frac{3}{4}$	$5\frac{7}{16}$	$16\frac{7}{16}$
	Back boards	$\frac{1}{2}$	17	30
	Top moulding	$\frac{3}{4}$	2	36

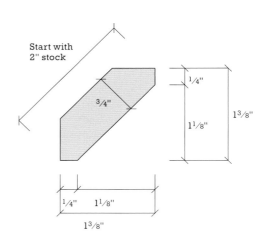

Here you can see how the bottom of the case acts as a door stop. This is one of the reasons I build my face frames first: I can make sure my bottom will be in perfect position.

Fit the face frame on the case. The stiles should hang $1/16$" over the edge of the case so you can rout (or plane) them flush later.

careful not to get any glue in the groove that holds the panel. When the glue is dry, hang the door in your face frame.

Finally, the Case

The case is simple. The top and bottom pieces fit into ¼"-deep dados and rabbets on the sides. The back rests in a rabbet on the sides and is nailed to the back edge of the top and bottom pieces.

You'll use your face frame to lay out your joints on the sides. You want the bottom piece to end up ³/₁₆" higher than the top edge of the bottom rail on your face frame. This allows your bottom to act as a stop for the door. Mark the location of that ¼"-deep dado and cut. The top piece rests in a ¼"-deep x ¾"-wide rabbet on the sides. Cut that using your table saw. Then cut the ½"-deep x ¼"-wide rabbet on the back edge of the sides.

Drill holes for shelf pins and space them 1" apart on the sides. Sand the inside of the case. You'll notice that the top and bottom are ½" narrower than the sides. This is to give you a good place to nail the back pieces to the case. Assemble the case using glue and nails, making sure the top, bottom and sides are all flush at the front.

Attach the face frame to the case using glue and nails. Trim the face frame flush to the case using a bearing-guided flush-cutting bit in your router. Finish sand the cabinet to #180-grit.

Take your scrap pieces and use them to make a shiplapped back. Cut a ¼" x ½" rabbet on the edges and then cut a bead on one edge using a ¼" beading bit in your router table. You want to give the back pieces room to expand and contract, about ⅛" between each board should be fine.

Cut the moulding for the top so it resembles the drawing detail at left. Finish sand everything, then nail the moulding to the top.

I like to peg the tenons in my doors to add a little strength. Drill a ¼" diameter hole most of the way through the stile and tenon. Then whittle a square piece of stock so it's round on one end, put glue in the hole and pound it in place. Cut the peg nearly flush. You want it to be a little proud of the stile – it's a traditional touch.

Break all the edges of the case with #120-grit sandpaper, and putty all your nail holes. Paint, dye or stain the all the components (I used a water-based aniline dye). Then add two coats of clear finish and nail the back pieces in place. Hang the cabinet by screwing through the back boards into a stud in your wall.

Supplies

Rockler
www.rockler.com; 800-279-4441
#31495 hinges for door, $8.99/pair

Horton Brasses Inc.
www.horton-brasses.com
800-754-9127
#K-12 w/MSF (machine screw fitting), check website or call for pricing

A Joiner's Tool Chest

BY ROY UNDERHILL

It's the modern joiner's dilemma. An old house over in the next county has missing mouldings on the mantel, a kicked-in panel on a bedroom door and seven sash with rotted rails. The question is: Do you lug your full tool chest to the site, or do you pick your planes and pack them in a satchel? The big chest needs four men to move it, and the satchel is a jumble. What you need, of course, is something midsized – you need a chest for the road.

This midsized chest is also a midsized challenge. The sides are common through-dovetails, but the skirt requires a few variations that will bring your dovetailing skills up a notch.

Equally important as the dovetails are the interlocking grooves – grooves that join the bottom into the skirt, the skirt into the broad sides and the panel into the frame of the lid. Even the miter-shouldered bridle joints in the corners of the lid are just overgrown tongue-and-

groove joints. The keystone to this chest is the interlock that joins the skirt to the sides. The skirt itself adds depth to the chest – without your having to glue up your stock edge-to-edge. With the narrower boards available these days, a deep dovetailed chest is usually made up from two or more boards glued edge to edge to make one broad one. But even when the joints are well executed, the built-up look of the sides is always disturbing.

Here though, after subtracting the 1½" overlap, joining the 5½" skirt to the 11¼" sides allows these readily available widths to add up to a 15¼"-deep chest.

The Gauge Rules

With all these long grooves (more than 38' by my measure), smart money would bet on the plow plane as the most valuable player. My vote would go instead to the double-toothed mortising gauge. The plow plane, making repeated passes and occasionally rocking over, tends to open

up. By the time you get to the last board, the fence has eased and the groove is farther in from the edge than you intended. By contrast, the mortising gauge makes only one pass down each board and easily holds its setting. The sharp teeth of the gauge also help the plow plane make a clean job by severing the grain at the surface. For that matter, if you are plowless at the moment, once you've scribed the lines with the gauge, you can cut all the grooves with chisels in short (well, medium) order.

As in drawer building, grooving comes before dovetailing. Set your mortising gauge to ¾" in and ¾" wide and run it down the lower face of the side-board stock and the upper back of the skirt-board stock. Plow the groove ¼" deep within these lines. Unless you have a very long bench, you'll need to crosscut the boards into shorter sections for the plowing. You can cut the side boards to their final length, but it's wise to leave each of

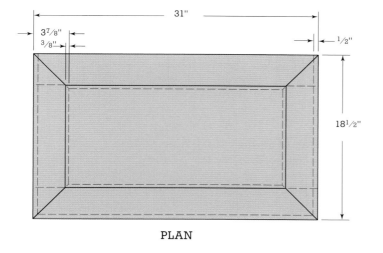

PLAN

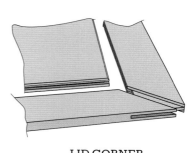

LID CORNER
JOINERY DETAIL

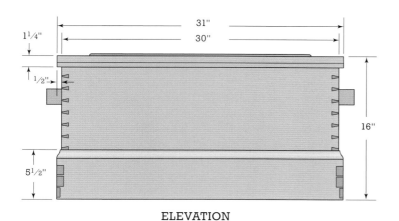

ELEVATION

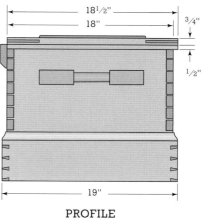

PROFILE

Pulling away this one piece of the skirt reveals all this chest's secrets.

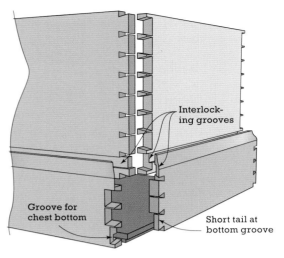

Interlock-ing grooves

Groove for chest bottom

Short tail at bottom groove

CORNER - EXPLODED VIEW

The first joinery is making the interlocking grooves in the pieces for the skirt and top section of the chest. Mark their locations with a mortising gauge first to increase your accuracy.

the four boards of the skirt an inch longer than needed – just in case.

I've dimensioned this chest so that the broad (expensive) side boards and top panel can be gotten out of a single 10' plank of pine or poplar. This gives you a chest 30" long by 18" wide, but if you want your 32"-long rip saw to fit inside, adjust accordingly.

Dovetail the Sides

Dovetails are strong in one direction and weak in the other, so it makes sense to orient them to resist the greatest load. In a tool chest that gets lifted and pulled along from the ends, the pins might logically go on the end boards. This also orients the attractive sloping face of the dovetails to the front of the chest. These days, the approved slope of dovetails has become beige and unthreatening – one in six (1:6) or so. But look at an old chest and the angle can be bold – up to

a frighteningly steep one in three (1:3). For a conservative 1:6 slope, no one will object if you make the pins equal to half the ¾" thickness of the wood at their widest point and the tails a bit less than twice the thickness of the wood. A steep slope will require bigger pins, because the slopes would converge before traversing the thickness of the wood. No matter the slope and spacing of the dovetails on the sides, treat the edge of the chest's interlock groove (which joins the skirt) as if it were the edge of the board, ending with half-pins as custom demands.

I'll assume you know how to cut the through-dovetails for the broad boards of the sides. If not, you can readily find this information elsewhere or derive my preferred method when we get to the skirt.

You may not need four people to lift this chest, but that's a good number to have around when you glue the sides. First, though, dry-fit the dovetails, push-

ing them at least halfway home. Pay close attention to the edges of the boards – the half pins are easily split away by a fat fit. Make any shims you'll need to fill miscuts and place them at the ready at each corner. Before you call in your helpers, set a box of doughnuts at the other end of the shop. Have everyone take a corner of the chest and paint on the glue. Squeeze up the sides with bar clamps, testing for equal diagonals to square the corners. Thank your helpers and send them off to eat the doughnuts – otherwise, they'll all want to help you tap in the shims. That is a job you need to do by yourself.

The Skirt

In a painted tool chest where the dovetails will not show as prominently, you might choose to orient the dovetails in the skirt counter to the ones in the chest sides. This is not pretty, but it's stronger and better resists the outward thrust of

Saw the miter in the skirt, but saw a little shy from your scribe line. You can tune up this joint later by laying a saw kerf through it.

The first cut with the dovetail saw below the miter is straight across the skirt.

an expanding bottom. In a varnished chest of nice wood living a less rough-and-tumble life, however, I'd orient the dovetails of the skirt and sides in the same direction.

The skirt-board stock already has one groove plowed into it for the interlock. It now needs a second groove, ⅜" wide and ⅜" in from the edge, to hold the rabbeted ¾" bottom. Plowing these grooves first helps you lay out the dovetails to cover them.

For the skirt joinery, it may help to think of each corner of the skirt as having two regions. The upper region is a simple butted miter joint that conceals the interlock groove and gives the moulding a neat corner. The lower region is dovetailed, with three tails and four pins. You could start in either area, but I'll begin with the miter because once you have cut it, the region for the dovetail is more clearly defined.

See that your ends are planed square and true. Set your cutting gauge to the thickness of the wood, plus 1⁄32", and mark all around the ends of both pieces.

Use the line scribed by the cutting gauge on the back sides as the origin for the 45° lines across the edges that define the miter joint. As always, you want to saw on the waste side of the line, but here you might choose to leave a bit more meat on each mitered face. That way, when you bring the joint closed, the mitered faces will hit before the dovetails fully seat. You'll then be able to "kerf in" and close the joint by sawing precisely down the seam. On a miter, you usually want to saw from the "inside out" so that you cut more with the flow of the grain. Once you have planed mouldings into the stock, however, you need to saw into the finished face to keep the edges from feathering. The mitered edges of the moulding are also quite sharp and easily damaged as you cut the dovetails. Leaving the mitered faces just a hair fat then kerfing them in at the finish helps protect them from damage.

Stand the piece chosen for the tails upright in the vise and square across the end grain precisely at the edge of the interlock groove. Carry this line down the face to the gauged line. Follow this line with your saw, working carefully to leave the interlock groove at its full width rather than letting the saw slip into the groove.

Lay out the dovetails using the diagonal rule method, positioning the rule to end at the centerlines of the spaces for the ending half-pins. Here, marks made every 1½" along the rule divide the dovetailed part of the skirt into three equal parts.

Measure out the width of the pin-spaces from the centerlines and draw the slopes down to the edge, guided by your bevel gauge. Note that the spaces of the half-pins are just as wide as those for the two full pins – they are "half" only in the sense of having a slope on but one cheek.

Stand the piece upright in the vise and carry these lines square across the end grain. Saw just the cheeks of the dovetails.

Remove this tail piece from the vise and stand the pin piece in its place, positioning its end flush with a plane laid on its side. Slide the plane back and set the tail piece spanning the two, carefully aligning the mark of the cutting gauge on the tail piece with the inside edge of the pin piece. Hold everything steady as you draw the dovetail saw back through each kerf, transferring the cut lines to the end grain of the pin piece.

Square the transferred lines down the face of the pin board to the gauged line.

A Joiner's Toolchest

NO.	ITEM	DIMENSIONS (INCHES) T	W	L	MATERIAL
2	Side panels	¾	11¼	30	Soft wood
2	End panels	¾	11¼	18	Soft wood
2	Short skirt parts	¾	5½	19	Soft wood
2	Long skirt parts	¾	5½	31	Soft wood
1	Bottom	¾	18	30¼	Soft wood
2	Long lid pieces	¾	3⅞	31	Soft wood
2	Short lid pieces	¾	3⅞	18½	Soft wood
1	Lid panel	¾	11½	24	Soft wood
	Dust lip	½	½	70	Soft wood
2	Handles	1¼	2	12	Hardwood

Angle your rule across the skirt to divide the remaining area into three parts.

Lay out the slopes of your tails from the centerlines you established with your rule.

The socket that houses the groove for the bottom is only half as deep as the other two and must be marked accordingly. Mark the end grain of the dovetail first, indicating the wood to pare away. Then, reset the cutting gauge to mark the depth of the socket by adding $\frac{1}{32}$" to the previous setting. This is all easier done than said.

Begin the pins by aligning your saw precisely with the waste side of the transfer marks and sawing down. Remember to saw only the inside diagonal of the cheek of the pin that coincides with the wall of the interlock groove. If you used too much pressure when transferring, the marks will be more like shallow grooves that try to pull your saw into them. Cut beside them, not in them.

Saw the mitered end, then saw out the bulk of the wood between the pins with your coping saw. Pare back to the gauge lines. On the final slice, set the chisel right in the cut made by the gauge.

Return to the dovetailed board and chisel out the spaces for the pins.

Saw and chisel the shallow dovetail flush to the line coinciding with the bottom of the groove.

When you push the skirt joint together, the miter should close just as, or just

Use your dovetail saw to scribe the pattern for your pins. Use light pressure. You don't want to plow a groove.

The first cut on your pin board defines the mitered area that will meet the tail board. It does not break through on the show side of the skirt.

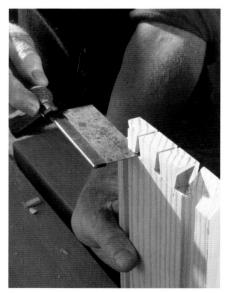

Saw out the shallow dovetail joint at the bottom of the skirt. See the illustrations for details on what this looks like.

If the miter closes before the dovetails, run your saw through the miter joint. Saw into the joint as shown to avoid feathering where the saw exits the miter.

Here I'm using a complex moulding plane on the skirt. Before moulding the skirt, remove the bulk of the waste with other tools.

before, the dovetails hit bottom. If you need to kerf in the miter, first see that the corner is square and firmly held. Saw right down the seam from the outside face with a fine saw and be sure to stop before you cut into the half pin of the dovetail. Pull the joint open, inspect the mating surfaces and remove any remaining wood with a chisel. Close the joint again and check the fit. Four surfaces in three different planes have to meet at the same time, so you see why I suggested leaving the skirt pieces an inch or more longer than needed – you'll have at least one chance to start over.

The decorative moulding around the top edge of the skirt might be a simple bevel or an ogee or something more complex, but such decorative touches are often well left for last so they won't get banged up. Just as with the grooves, it's best to lay out the moulding with a gauge before planing. Here though, any sharp scribing points would leave their traces, so a pencil gauge or pencil divider is the ticket. Following these pencil lines, rough in the moulding with a drawknife and gouge, and use the moulding plane to bring it home.

The skirt has to fit around the waist of the chest, bottoming into the interlock. Too loose and the glue surfaces won't meet. Too tight and the skirt joints won't close. Don't glue any corners until you have fitted it all around (and inserted the bottom!). If the skirt is a bit tight, you can plane shavings from the faces of the interlock all around to make it sit a little deeper. If one broad side of the chest has the best looking wood and joinery, see if you can turn the skirt so that it too puts its "best face to London."

Bottoming

A good bottom should fit neatly inside the skirt, tight enough to stay in place but loose enough to allow movement. At some point your chest is going to sit on damp concrete or wet grass and its bottom is going to expand. This is when joining cheaper boards with tongues and grooves makes your bottom better. These joints can absorb some of the movement and prevent an expanding bottom from pushing the skirt dovetails apart.

First, join the bottom boards with tongues and grooves into an assembly that is larger than it needs to be. Gauge lines ¼" in on one long-grain side and ⅜" in on one end-grain side. Set the chest with its dry-fitted skirt on the bottom and align the inner edges with these gauged lines. Trace the remaining two lines on the bottom and mark it and the skirt so they can be reassembled in the same orientation. Lift off the chest and add ¼" to the new lines on the bottom. Saw and plane the bottom to these lines. Flip the bottom over and use a rabbet plane or moving fillister plane to leave a ⅜"-square tongue all around. In the end, the bottom will fit only ¼" into the side grooves, leaving ⅛" for expansion. Because the bottom boards won't expand along their length, the end-grain tongues on the bottom can fit more deeply in their grooves.

Insert the bottom and check the

A tongue-and-groove joint in your bottom boards ensures the longevity of your chest.

dry-fit of the skirt all around. Glue the interlock grooves and the skirt dovetails. You might use a dab of glue at the center of the end grain of each bottom board, but otherwise leave the bottom dry. Before the glue sets, burnish the mitered mouldings shut with the smooth back of a gouge. After the glue sets, plane off that last protruding ⅟₃₂".

The Lid

The grooves and joints that connect the frame and panel of the lid all begin as lines made by the mortising gauge. The gauge lines define the grooving and the grooving defines the joints. It's easy to see how the sockets of the miter-shouldered bridle joints are just extensions of the groove, but the grooves define the tenons as well. Plowing the grooves removes some of the potential width of the tenons, something you may discover too late if you work out of sequence. Start with the gauge, plow the grooves and work on from there.

Tenon the Long

The tenons of the lid frame go on the long front boards so that the end grain shows only on the side edges of the lid. Mark the face sides of all your pieces and run the mortising gauge around the inner edges and the ends. Plow the

With the groove already cut by the plow, the tenons' cheeks are easy to define with a saw.

Use the newly cut tenon to define the depth of the mortise in the short rails of the lid.

groove within these lines. Saw the shoulders of the tenon in a miter box if you have one. Split and pare away the waste wood on either side of the groove and run the gauge down the newly exposed wood to more clearly mark the thickness of the tenon. Now you can stand the end upright in the vise and saw the tenon cheeks without the saw pulling into the

groove. This finished tenon now defines the width of the mortise.

Mortise the Short

Lay the tenon over the mitered end of the short piece and trace the breadth of its overlap. The mortise of the bridle joint is easy enough to cut out with a rip saw, chisel and rasp, but the plow plane

A miter box makes accurate work of the tenons' mitered shoulders.

By beginning to make the mortise with a plow, you create a guide for your saw.

Dust lip

Underside of panel

Here you can see how the pieces to the lid come together with the panel. Be sure to allow for some expansion when figuring the width of the panel.

The tool chest's handles are each turned and then sawn from one piece of stout hardwood.

can start the job. Plow a groove down the sloping end grain on the miters and down the short outer face of the mortise and you'll create a nice shoulder for the saw to ride against. Here's where the gauged lines rule once more. Because you can only plane down a slope, not up, you'll occasionally have to turn the wood around and fence from its back side. Unless the groove is dead center, you'll have to make a slight adjustment to the fence on the plane. Because working within the gauged lines keeps everything aligned in the same plane, you can safely adjust the plane as needed.

Place the Panel

Dry-fit the frame together, then measure the opening to find the size of the panel. As with the bottom, the panel can fit fully in the groove at its ends, but the sides need room to expand. If the ¼"-wide groove in both the frame and the panel is ⅜" deep, measure the panel to overlap the opening in the frame by only ¼" on the sides. This will leave room for the panel to shrink and swell over a range of ½" without becoming loose or tight.

Joinery for the chest ends with gluing the lid-frame corners with the dry-fitted panel in place – the rest of the work is connected with fasteners. Hinge the lid with two or three butts and screw a ¾" x 3" x 30" stop to the back of the chest to keep the lid from falling all the way back. Glue and screw a ½"-square lip around the front and sides of the lid, mitering the meeting ends and leaving just enough

room for the lid to open and close snugly. You've done such a careful job so far, do take the time to track down proper straight-slotted steel screws.

Handles

The turned and sawn handles are smaller versions of ones found on an 1830s-vintage American tool chest. Each begins as a 12" length of 1¼" x 2" white oak, ash or maple. Set it in the lathe with the centers at ⅝" in from the edge. Turning such unbalanced wood is dangerous so keep it slow. You might want to saw some of the stock away to reduce the wobble and time on the lathe. When the grip is finished, cut out the curves with a turning saw and chamfer the edges with a spokeshave.

The handles take a heavy load, so it

won't do to simply screw them onto the thin end boards. Use multiple screws from inside and out. If your tool chest will have tills sliding on hard wooden rails fastened to the inside ends, plan ahead and move the handles up or down to take advantage of this solid anchorage.

So that's it. Locks and interior fittings are where you can really strut your stuff – or not. My chest just has two rough sliding tills and a till for moulding planes. Fastened to the underside of my lid you'll find a saw and some naughty postcards in a space that will forever go begging for fine marquetry. It's well-traveled, battered and blue. Over time, I expect that your chest will come to reflect you, too.

Stay sharp.

Cherry Wall Cabinet

BY MATTHEW TEAGUE

Through the early stages of my woodworking, when I was sweating away evenings in a Mississippi basement trying to learn the craft using a $99 table saw and an $18 block plane, I devoured the books of James Krenov. They represented an artistic, if idealized, approach to a hands-on craft that appealed to an angst-filled editor and writer in his 20s. Even if I wasn't up to the tasks, I knew my aim. Then life took over. After editing, writing and running a furniture business for a number of years, I still looked at the Krenov books from time to time, but my tastes and styles slowly became my own. When I started this job, however, I was inspired to revisit Krenov and the designs that kept me wide-eyed in earlier days. I'm glad I did.

I can't tell you how many Sam Maloof-style rockers or knockoffs of Brian Boggs Appalachian ladderbacks I've seen over the years, only to have their makers look me straight in the face and tell me how they came up with their "original" design. With that in mind, I can't claim that any significant design decision in this piece belongs to anyone other than Krenov.

I've only built a few actual reproduction pieces in my life, and while this can't be called a strict reproduction, it's about as close as I get. Most times I either come up with something from my head or look through designs from numerous makers and periods until some amalgamation thereof seems to stick. This piece, however, evolved slightly differently.

As I set out to design a small, two-door wall cabinet, I looked through various woodworking and furniture books – Krenov's and otherwise. As usual, I studied numerous designs, then put them aside and started scribbling away at a sketch pad.

Once you've been exposed to good ideas, however, they're a little hard to shake. While it wasn't my original intention, time and time again, I found myself returning to design touches I'd seen on a particular Krenov display cabinet. Though at times unconventional, a few of Krenov's design solutions seemed so obvious after I saw them that I was unable to return to something more traditional.

Tapered Sliding Dovetails

Because the case will be dry-fit and reassembled multiple times, tapered sliding dovetails are a good choice because they don't bind or even close up until the very end of the joint. Once closed, however, tapered sliding dovetails are strong mechanical joints that need only a few drops of glue to secure them in place. They're also an ideal joint for bookcases and other instances where long joints are needed. To cut them, all you need is a router, dovetail bit, right-angle guide, a loose length of plywood to use as a fence and a shim.

Cut a tapered dovetail slot by shimming out the leading edge of the guide fence and recutting the dovetail slot.

With the same dovetail bit partially buried in the fence, cut a tapered tail by attaching the same shim material to the rear outer edge of the side stock.

Remove stock from the tail stock gradually, testing the fit until it slides snugly into the slot.

This striking but seemingly straightforward display cabinet is a design that Krenov built a few times over the years. The first iteration was made of Swedish ash and appeared in his first book, "A Cabinetmaker's Notebook" (Van Nostrand Reinhold), and a later version made of Andaman padauk appeared in "Worker in Wood" (Sterling). Krenov built these cabinets in slightly different sizes, but all shared a few essential features: the angled case and doors; center

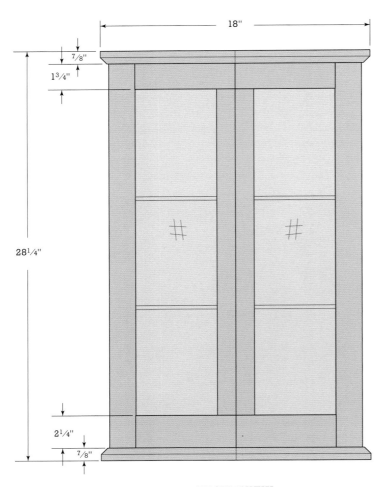

FRONT VIEW

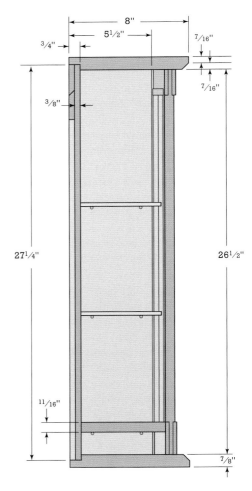

SECTION VIEW

Cherry Wall Cabinet

NO.	ITEM	DIMENSIONS (INCHES)			MATERIAL
		T	W	L	
1	Top*	$7/8$	8	18	Cherry
1	Bottom*	$7/8$	8	18	Cherry
2	Sides**	$3/4$	$5^5/8$	$27^1/2$	Cherry
2	Upper door rails†	$3/4$	$1^3/4$	$8^5/8$	Cherry
2	Lower door rails†	$3/4$	$2^1/4$	$8^5/8$	Cherry
2	Outer door stiles	$3/4$	$1^7/8$	$26^1/2$	Cherry
2	Inner door stiles	$5/8$	$1^1/4$	$26^1/2$	Cherry
1	Cabinet back††	$3/8$	$15^7/8$	$27^1/4$	Cherry
2	French cleats	$3/8$	$2^1/2$	$7^1/2$	Cherry
1	Lower shelf	$1^1/16$	$5^3/8$	$15^3/8$	Cherry
2	Upper shelves	$1/4$	$5^3/8$	$15^3/8$	Glass
2	Door panels	$3/16$	$6^5/16$	$23^3/8$	Glass
2	Pulls	$5/8$	$5/8$	1	Walnut

* Leave 2" long until after routing the sliding dovetail. ** Left slightly wide at this point – trim to final angle after dry-fitting.

† Leave $1/8$" longer, to be trimmed to finished size after. †† Glue up boards as necessary to span width.

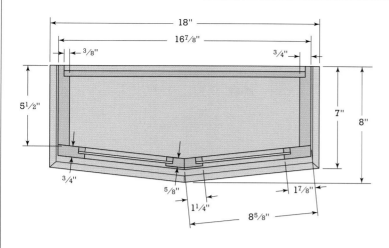

TOP VIEW

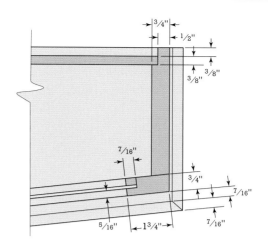

CORNER DETAIL

stiles that are recessed and visible only between the rails (rather than the traditional arrangement); and backs made up of bookmatched boards that create an interesting but not overpowering pattern.

In Krenov's spirit of working with what the wood gives you, my own cabinet is slightly larger in all dimensions and more squat in proportions. And while I never put a scale to Krenov's door parts, I let my eye steal what it could. The doors are built using bridle joints and hung on straight knife hinges, both of which are common in Krenov's work.

As for the case, the edge profiles on the top and bottom are more angular and hard-edged on my piece than the originals, and the case joinery is a little different. I can only assume that Krenov assembled the cases using dowel joints, his go-to joint for case construction. I opted for tapered sliding dovetails instead. And though they have the reputation of being fussy, the knife hinges used to hang the doors are actually straightforward and easily installed – you just have to make sure you plan for them before you assemble the case.

A Case for Tapered Sliding Dovetails

Many techniques would work for building this case; it could be biscuited, screwed and plugged, or, Krenov's choice, assembled using dowel joints. Because it's a more familiar route, I chose tapered sliding dovetails, a strong mechanical joint that works well in cases like this

where the top and bottom overhang the sides. While a cabinet of this depth could be assembled using traditional sliding dovetails, the tapered version allows you to easily assemble and disassemble the case numerous times as you test the fit of the hinges.

To rout tapered sliding dovetails you need only a simple right-angle guide, a piece of scrap to work as an adjustable fence and a shim roughly ¹⁄₁₆" thick. Create the right-angle guide out of plywood scrap by screwing a short, straight length of plywood (about 2" wide x 10" long) square to the edge of a larger scrap – about 4" x 10". To cut the dovetail slot use a ½"-wide by ½"-long dovetail bit (mine is 14°) set to full depth in your router.

After jointing and planing the stock to thickness, leave the top and bottom an extra 2" long so that your router has more support as you cut the tapered sliding dovetails. Align the router bit with the centerline for the slot on the top and bottom. Clamp both the right-angle guide and the adjustable fence in place. You can make the cut in a single pass but it causes less strain on the bit and less trepidation for the user if you hog out the bulk of the waste using a ³⁄₁₆" straight bit before routing the dovetail slot. Mark out and stop the slot about ½" shy of the finished depth of the side. Make this same hogging cut for all of the dovetail slots. Then switch to the dovetail bit and repeat the cut. To make sure you position the fence in the same location for both the hogging

and dovetailing passes, align the guides using a combination square registered off the end.

After your first pass with the dovetail bit, position your shim along the edge of the workpiece between the guide and the adjustable fence. Make sure the end of the fence is positioned at the point on the bottom or top where the cabinet side ends. To open up one side of the dovetail slot and create a tapered dovetail slot, run the router against the shimmed fence. Then square up the end of the dovetail slot using a chisel.

Cut the dovetails on the ends of the case sides by chucking the same bit in the router table and setting the depth to match the depth of the dovetail slot in the top and bottom. (This is where it pays to make test cuts in scrap stock milled to the thickness of the case parts.) Use masking tape to attach the same shim used to cut the dovetail slot to the outside face of the side stock so that it is flush to the back edge. Alternate taking passes on each side of the stock, slowly adjusting the fence toward the bit until the tail fits snugly in the dovetail slot. Because both the dovetail and its mating slot are tapered, the fit will be loose until it seats itself to full depth. (The fat end of the dovetail should match the opening in the dovetail slot.)

Once you're happy with the fit, crosscut the top and bottom to length and then cut the angled front edges at the band saw. Clamp the two parts together and clean up the cut with a handplane.

Exposed Joinery for the Doors

Bridle joints, often called slip joints, are a little easier to cut than traditional mortise-and-tenon joints because all the door parts get cut to full length, which you can check directly against the case. The joinery is also exposed, which lends a handcrafted look to the piece.

Using a tall fence and a right-angle guide, center the mortise by taking two passes – one with either face against the fence – using a single blade.

Set the blade to match the thickness of the mortise walls. Then use a stop-block on a table saw sled to cut the tenon shoulder.

Trim away both sides of the tenon, testing the fit and making slight adjustments after each pass.

Aim for a tenon that slides into the mortise with a little resistance using only hand pressure.

Use a 45° chamfer bit at the router table to profile the edges of the top and bottom. Just make sure you don't chamfer past the point where the cabinet sides meet the faces of the top and bottom.

Streamlined Doormaking

Bridle joints are a handsome exposed joint that puts the maker's work on display. Using them to join the doors makes the fitting process almost foolproof. Start with stock that fits the opening and then cut your joinery. As long as you glue up the door square, it's essentially pre-fit to the case. Bridle joints are also straightforward: All you need is a tall auxiliary fence for your table saw and a right-angle guide to help hold the workpieces safely.

The rail and stile arrangement for these doors is simple, but certainly not traditional. The outer stiles run full length, as is traditional, but the inner stiles are inset and visible only between the upper and lower rails. To make the process easy, cut all the joinery on stock that is milled to the same thickness. After the joinery has been cut, the front face of the center stiles are run through the planer again so that their faces are set back ⅛" from the rail faces.

This arrangement allows the top and bottom rails to come to a point at center, highlighting the angled front of the case. It also creates an almost visually seamless frame around the cabinet, which helps draw your eyes to the inside of the case and creates an interesting shadow line reminiscent of Greene & Greene. I like it, but if the doors don't fit your tastes, feel free to build the doors with the more traditional arrangement.

Start by cutting all your stock to finished length, aiming for about ⅟32" of play top-to-bottom. Remember that angles will be trimmed on the stiles after the door is assembled – so cut the stock about 3⁄16" wider than finished width. It helps guide your milling to draw out the door parts to size on the bottom of the dry-fit case. You can always trim down doors that are too large, but there's no saving doors that are too small.

Start by cutting the open mortises on the outer stiles and on the inner ends of the rails. For each joint, set the height of the blade to match the width of the mating piece. It makes sense to cut them in batches based on the depth of cut. Position the workpiece upright in a right-angle sled held against the tall fence. Adjust the blade so that it cuts about ¼" in from the edge and make the cut. To prevent burning, make these cuts in two passes. You'll want to make this cut on all four joints before raising the blade to final height. Flip the stock so that the opposite face is against the fence and repeat the cut. Taking two passes with a single blade rather than one pass with a dado stack ensures that the mortise is centered on the stock. Depending on your saw blade, you may need to clean up the end of the mortise with a chisel.

Before cutting the tenon cheeks, cut their shoulders with the stock held flat on the table saw and registered against a miter gauge or a crosscut sled outfitted with a stop block set to the tenon length. Cut the tenon cheeks using a setup similar to the one you used for mortising, but with the blade adjusted to remove the faces of the stock. Sneak up on the fit slowly by taking passes on each side. Test the fit against the mortise and aim for a joint that is snug but can be assembled with only hand pressure.

After all the joinery is cut, run the center stiles through the planer, trimming their front faces down by about ⅛". Assemble the doors on a flat surface and make sure the assembly goes together square by measuring the diagonals. The two measurements should match.

Knife Hinges Lend a Clean Look

Many woodworkers steer clear of knife hinges, assuming that they're too difficult to fit correctly. But they're needlessly daunted. Knife hinges are nearly impossible to install if you attempt to do so on a case that has already been assembled, but if you plan for them prior to assembly they're pretty straightforward. They also add minimal visual distraction to the case, putting the design, the joinery and the wood itself on display.

Start by drawing out the location of the hinges on the top and bottom of the case. Dry-fit the case and position a scrap of the door stock against the front edge of the cabinet side; to give it a little breathing room, shim it out by the thickness of a business card. Then find the centerline of the door stock and transfer the location of the hinge.

Center one hinge leaf on the line and hold or tape it in place. Set a combination square so that when it's positioned against the front of the bottom it abuts the front edge of the hinge. Butt the hinge against the square and position it so that the inside edge of the pivot is flush to the outside edge of the case. (It's worth noting that on cases without angled fronts, the pivot of the knife hinge is centered on the outer edge of the case.) Once you're happy with the position of the hinge leaf, use double-sided tape to help hold the hinge in place and scribe a line around its perimeter. Disassemble the case and duplicate these markings for the remaining three hinges.

Use a ⅛" straight router bit that is set to the thickness of one leaf of the knife hinge (the same set up used to mortise the top and bottom). Clamp or use double-sided tape to secure an edge guide to the bottom of your router so that the bit aligns with the rear edge of the hinge mortise. You could use a plunge router to cut the mortise, but I find I get more consistent results using a fixed-base version and dropping carefully into the cut. Work the router in small circles, freehand, to hog off the bulk of the waste. Then take a final pass with the guide fence flush to the front of the workpiece to establish the rear edge of the mortise. Remove as much waste as you're comfortable removing freehand, and then clean up the edges of the mortise with a chisel.

Screw the leaves of the hinges (make sure it's the side of the hinge that has a pin and washer on it) into their mortises and reassemble the case. Make sure you drill the pilot holes and use steel screws. You can install the brass screws later but they tend to break unless you first thread the holes with steel ones.

Supplies

Brusso
brusso.com or 212-337-8510

2 center pivot hinges (aka knife hinges) #ST-18, $26.40/pair

Price correct at time of publication.

Installing Knife Hinges

Knife hinges work well in cases where you want minimal intrusion from the hardware. Straight knife hinges, like those seen here, are used on cabinets where the top and bottom of the case overhangs the door but the door overlays the case sides. The key to installing them without incident is to do all your mortising and test-fitting before gluing up the case.

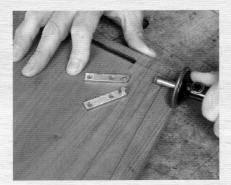

Draw out the position of the door stock to help center the hinge. Then use a marking gauge to establish the front and rear edges of the hinge mortise.

Use double-sided tape to hold the hinge in place and then scribe its location with a marking knife.

Hog out the waste in the mortise using a small straight bit. Position the edge guide so it makes a clean cut along the rear edge of the mortise.

The hinge leaf should be flush to the surface of the workpiece. Drill pilot holes before attaching it with screws.

Scrap stock clamped flush to the top of the door allows you to rout the door mortises in the same fashion as those on the case.

Attach the hinge leaves to the cabinet and one side of the door. Set the leaf attached to the door in place on the hinge. Set the other leaf in place on its hinge and slide the door into place. Double-check the position of the door on the case and then mark out the screw holes. Finish the doors and install the glass before you attach the doors permanently.

Finish up the Doors & Case

At the table saw, cut the angles on the edges of the assembled doors so that they fit snug between the hinge washers on the top and bottom of the case. Determine the length of the mortise so that the bit matches the distance mortised on the case (from the outside edge moving in toward the center). Then hold or tape the hinge in place and mark the end of the cut with a knife.

Set a combination square or marking gauge and scribe lines on the sides of the hinge so that it is perfectly centered. Clamp the door upright to the side of your bench or in a vise and clamp a guide block flush to the edge of the door. Attach a guide fence to the router base so that it aligns with the far edge of the mortise. Flip the door horizontally and cut the other edge of the mortise. Routing from both sides of the door guarantees that the mortise is perfectly centered on the door. Repeat this for the remaining mortises.

Set the mating hinge leaf on the hinges at the top and bottom of the case and then slide the door into place so that the hinge leaves slide into the door mortises. If the door needs to set farther in, you can open up the ends of the mortises on the doors. Once you're happy with the position of the doors on the hinges, drill the screw holes. You can install the leaf in one end of the door (either the top or the bottom), but leave the other loose so that you can slide it onto the hinge in the case.

Before attaching the doors permanently you need to glue up the case then apply your favorite finish (I used Waterlox). Route a $^{7}/_{16}$"-wide by $^{3}/_{8}$"-deep rabbet on the inside edges of the door then square up the corners. Use a small bead of silicone and install wood strips to secure the glass in place.

To finish up the case, drill for shelf pins. You can position them wherever you like or to fit the contents you plan to keep in the case. In my own cabinet I installed a lower wooden shelf that sits flush with the top of the lower door rail. This prevents the contents of the cabinet from being hidden behind the door rail. The upper shelves are ¼" glass.

The back of the cabinet is a good spot to highlight a few bookmatched or especially figured boards you've been holding on to for awhile. Rabbet the back of the case about ¾" deep and ⅜" wide and then install the ⅜"-thick back. You can shiplap the boards or glue them up as one solid panel, as I did.

To hang the cabinet, attach a French cleat to the back – simply a 5"-wide board ripped down the center at 45°. The upper length attaches to the back of the case and the lower section mounts to the wall.

My pulls differ from Krenov's. I band sawed them to shape and then refined them with a carving knife.

Throughout building this cabinet I was reminded of a story Hunter S. Thompson told: He claims to have once typed out the entirety of F. Scott Fitzgerald's "The Great Gatsby" simply to know how it felt to type those words. After completing essentially the same task with Krenov's display cabinet I'm convinced that Thompson's pursuit wasn't as crazy as it sounds. At least this one.

A departure from Krenov's original, the gently curved walnut pulls emphasize the vertical lines of the doors.

A bead of silicone and wood strips secure the glass in place. Use cardboard to protect the glass as you tap the brads home.

Chimney Cupboard

BY MEGAN FITZPATRICK & GLEN D. HUEY

There's a backstory to this chimney-cupboard project. Last March, I planned a week off to renovate the 6½' x 8' bathroom in my 110-year-old house (I was sure it wouldn't take long – after all, I only had to gut it to the studs and joists, hang new drywall, reroute plumbing …). Three months later, I finally had the tile in and grouted, and a working shower. A month after that, I installed a medicine cabinet and put up the wainscoting and the trim. So close on a year later, I'm almost done. But the small space allowed no room for built-in storage, and I was unwilling to tear out adjoining plaster walls to enlarge the space.

So I needed a tall, free-standing cabinet that fit with my amalgamation of Victorian and Arts & Crafts design elements, and it had to fit into the narrow area between the shower door and commode, making the most use of available space. This three-drawer chimney cupboard was designed to accommodate a variety of storage needs, and fit a specific location. At 10½" the depth, due to space limitations, is fairly shallow. And, I wanted the piece to match the exact height of the shower wall, 78½" (I've been told I can be a tad persnickety). The point (yes, I do have one) is that it's easy to start with a design idea in mind, and adjust the dimensions and design elements such as inset versus lipped drawers, or hardware and mouldings, to meet your specific needs.

This tall chimney cabinet is perfect for any narrow space, whether in the kitchen, bath or elsewhere in your home.

First Steps

Before heading to the shop, we first designed the project in Google SketchUp (sketchup.com), a powerful (and free) design program that allows you to build in virtual space and get all the elements and measurements just as you want them (the files for this project are available at popularwoodworking.com/feb08).

Then, based on the measurements established in the drawings, we headed to the shop and pulled rough maple planks from our rack, selecting straight-grained boards for the face frame and side panels, and laid out the various elements. We rough cut the pieces to length for the face frame pieces and sides, adding 1" to the final lengths, then milled the stock to ¾" on the jointer and through the planer.

Face First: Mortise-and-Tenon

This is a face-frame cabinet, so building that frame is the initial step in the process. By completing it first, you can then use the finished frame to make any necessary size adjustments to the other pieces.

At the table saw, we ripped the rails, stiles and drawer dividers from the same S4S board, and crosscut them to final length. Then it was on to laying out the mortises on the rails.

Determine the face of each frame member, then clamp the stiles together with the working edge facing up. Use the drawing to locate each rail and divider along the length of the stiles and mark the top and bottom edge of each rail with a line completely across each stile. Next, move in a ½" from the top end of the stiles and draw a line setting the location of the mortise for the top rail. Move toward the center of each layout area ¼" and place a partial line for each of the remaining rails. Mortise only between these partial lines.

Using ¾" stock makes this a simple process. Set up a marking gauge to find the center of the workpiece. Using the marking gauge you've already set up, strike the centerline of one of your mortises (you'll use that mark to line up the bit at the mortiser).

You're now ready to make the cuts. Chuck a ¼" hollow-chisel mortising bit

in the mortiser, set the depth for 1¼" (setting the depth of cut on the strong side), then line up the bit point with the centerline you marked in the top mortise. Bore a series of holes across the mortise, leaving a little less than ¼" in between each hole (this helps to keep the chisel from deflecting). Go back and clean out the remaining waste, then make another series of passes from end to end in the mortise to clean out any remaining waste, and to break up any large chips (this will make it easier to knock out the sawdust). Then move on to the next mortise. Because each mortise is centered on your ¾" stock, you can flip the workpiece end-to-end and the setup will remain consistent.

With all your mortises cut, it's time to move on to the tenons on the rails. Again, ¾" stock makes it easy to center the tenons in your workpieces, and not have to change setups or spend much time measuring. Glen suggests using ¾" stock for all face frames when possible; that way the layout becomes second nature.

Each tenon is 1¼" in length and ¼" in thickness. Raise the blade in your table saw to just a hair under ¼". Set your fence at 1¼" to the outside edge of the blade, and make the cuts on all four shoulders of each end of each rail. Raise the blade to ½" when cutting the edge shoulder cut on the top rail. We used a tenon jig to cut the shoulders. Your fence setting will vary depending on your jig, but the idea is to leave a matching ¼" tenon when finished, with the blade raised to 1¼".

Cut the shoulder off the outside of the rail to keep from trapping waste material between the blade and the rail. It's a good idea to check the fit of that tenon in your mortises to see if you need to make any slight adjustments in your saw settings before you finish the rest of the cheek cuts. The goal is a snug fit. You should be able to insert the tenon into the mortise using hand pressure and maybe a little mallet tap – if too much force (or too little) is necessary, you'll want to adjust your fence accordingly.

Once you have that right, make the rest of your cheek cuts then head to the band saw to remove the remain-

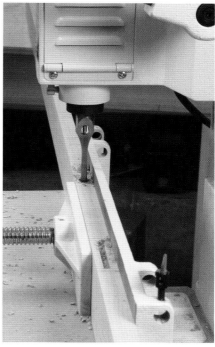

To ensure you get a nice, squared mortise, first make a series of cuts spaced a little less than $^1/_4$" apart; this will help keep the chisel from deflecting.

ing waste. Set up your fence a heavy ¼" from the outside edge of the blade so you're cutting away waste on the inside of each tenon (that way you can just flip the piece to make the second cut, without having to adjust the fence). This will make each tenon just a little loose from top to bottom in the mortise, allowing room for minor adjustments. Exercise caution to get the depth of your cut just right – if you cut past the proper depth, the kerf will show on your finished frame.

Supplies

Horton Brasses

800-754-9127 or
horton-brasses.com

2 Hinges (#PB-407B; satin nickel)

3 Bin pulls (#BN-2; satin nickel)

1 Door latch (#SL-4; satin nickel)

1 Clout nails (#N-7; 1/4 pound; 53 nails)

Make all four cuts on one end of each rail at the table saw, using a sled or sliding table.

This tenon jig keeps the workpiece secure as you cut off the cheeks of your tenons.

Chimney Cupboard

NO.	ITEM	DIMENSIONS (INCHES)			MATERIAL	
		T	W	L		
2	Face frame stiles	$3/4$	$2^3/4$	78	Maple	
1	Top face frame rail	$3/4$	$5^1/2$	18	Maple	$1^1/4$ TBE*
1	Bottom face frame rail	$3/4$	3	18	Maple	$1^1/4$ TBE
3	Face frame drawer dividers	$3/4$	$1^1/4$	18	Maple	$1^1/4$ TBE
2	Sides	$3/4$	$9^3/4$	78	Maple	
1	Top	$3/4$	9	20	Maple	
1	Fixed shelf	$3/4$	9	20	Maple	
3	Drawer extensions	$3/4$	$1^1/4$	$19^1/2$	Maple	
6	Drawer runners	$3/4$	$2^3/4$	$7^3/4$	Maple	$1/2$ TOE*
6	Drawer guides	$3/4$	$3/4$	8	Maple	
1	Nailing strip for backboards	$3/4$	$2^3/4$	$19^1/2$	Maple	
2	Door stiles	$3/4$	2	44	Maple	
1	Top door rail	$3/4$	$2^1/4$	14	Maple	$1^1/4$ TBE
1	Bottom door rail	$3/4$	$2^3/4$	14	Maple	$1^1/4$ TBE
	Back	$5/8$	$20^1/2$	78	Maple	
1	Top drawer front	$7/8$	4	$15^3/8$	Maple	
1	Middle drawer front	$7/8$	5	$15^3/8$	Maple	
1	Bottom drawer front	$7/8$	6	$15^3/8$	Maple	
1	Top frame front	$1/2$	$2^1/8$	$23^3/4$	Maple	45° ABE*
2	Top frame sides	$1/2$	$2^1/8$	$11^7/8$	Maple	45° AOE*
1	Top frame back	$1/2$	$2^7/8$	$19^1/2$	Maple	
1	Front crown	$13/16$	2	$22^5/8$	Maple	
2	Side crowns	$13/16$	2	$11^5/16$	Maple	
2	Long retainer strips	$5/16$	$5/16$	$39^3/4$	Maple	
2	Short retainer strips	$5/16$	$5/16$	$11^3/8$	Maple	

* TBE, Tenon both ends; TOE, Tenon one end; AOE, Angle both ends; AOE, Angle one end

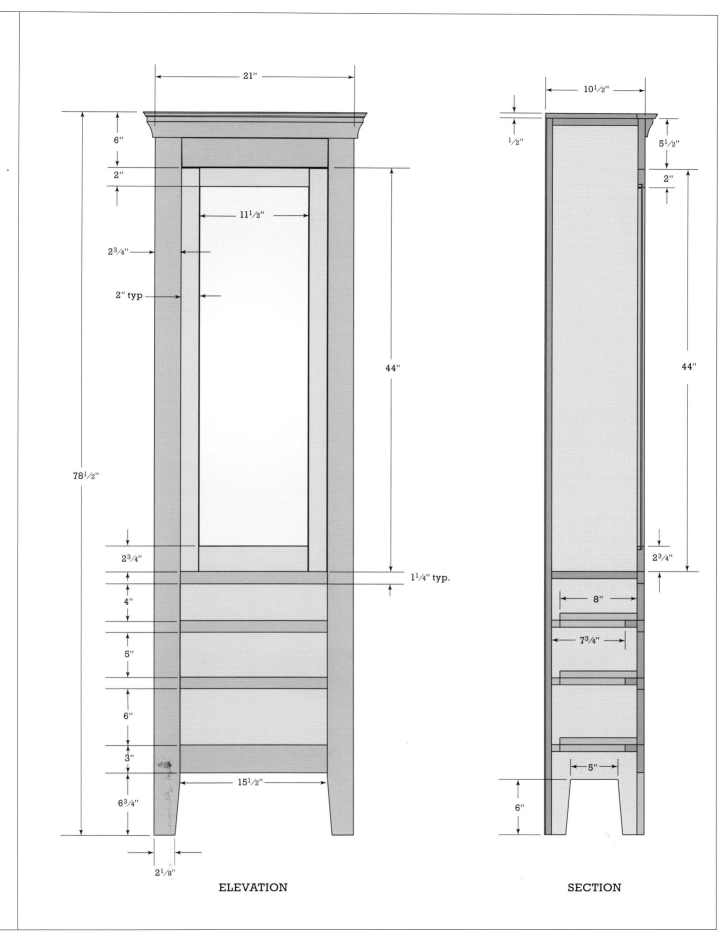

ELEVATION

SECTION

Dry-fit, Then Glue

Now dry-fit the frame together, and when everything looks good, take it back apart and squeeze glue into the mortises of all stiles, using an acid brush to coat all the surfaces. Then spread a thin layer of glue on the face of each tenon and mate the two. Remember: you left a little wiggle room on the mortise from top to bottom, so you can knock it one way or the other as necessary so that all your openings are square. Now do the same on the other side, check all the openings for square, and clamp it together to dry.

How much glue? Glen suggests that you look for a little bit of squeeze-out, so you know you've got enough. You can clean it up after it dries with a chisel or card scraper, or wipe it off while wet with a rag and warm water (though there is some argument that this could give you finishing problems later).

With everything squared up and fitting, add glue and clamp your face frame together and set it aside to dry.

Side Panels

Because the side panels have to be glued up from two pieces (unless you're lucky enough to find wide stock), it's important to take a close look at the pieces you're using, and work with any grain patterns and color variation to get the best-looking panels possible. I wanted the panel seam to be dead center, so I ripped from both edges of my surfaced boards to get the best look, and took the final passes for the glue line at the jointer. We then glued the panels and set them aside to dry.

With the panels dry, we lined up the top edges and marked the dado location at the top drawer divider (behind which is a ¾" solid shelf) then routed a ¾"-wide x ¼"-deep dado in each side panel using a shopmade straightedge guide for the router. We also routed a rabbet of the same size at the top end of the side panels to accept the top. We then moved to the table saw to cut a ¾" x ⁷⁄₁₆" two-step rabbet at the back edge of each side panel, to later receive shiplapped backboards. The ¾" flat cut is made first. I used a featherboard to help support and secure the second cut; for me, it's hard to hold a 9¾" piece of stock steady though a 78" long

cut without it moving.

Before gluing the sides to the face frame, we used a plywood jig we made at the drill press to drill ½" deep x ¼" holes for shelf pins to hold the three glass adjustable shelves (you could instead buy a plastic shelf-pin jig, or use peg board as a template.)

Then, we stuck a ¾" offcut into the dado, both to check the fit and to use it as a guide to line up the dado location with the top drawer divider, ran a bead of glue along the edge of the side panel, then clamped the panel and face frame flush. After it was dry, we did the same on the

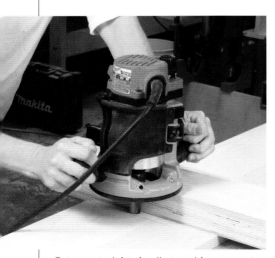

Set up a straightedge jig to guide your router through your shelf-groove cut.

This two-step rabbet cut is made more secure and safe by using a featherboard to help hold the workpiece.

Chucking an offcut into the shelf dado makes it easy to line up the face frame with the sides.

Make sure everything is lined up flush before tightening down the clamps. Secure the ends first, then adjust as necessary through the middle to compensate for any slight bowing.

opposite side. We then made a template for the side cutouts, clamped it to the bottom edge of the side panel, and used a ¼" top-bearing router bit to cut out the shape on both sides after trimming it with a jigsaw.

Next, we cut and fit the shelf and case top into the side/face frame assembly. The shelf is held with 1¼" brads installed from below the shelf, into the side panels; the top is attached with brads coming in from the top.

Next up were the drawer extensions, the runners and the drawer guides. Cut the extensions according to the cut sheet and fit each to the case directly behind the top edge of the dividers. Before they are glued in place you'll need to create the ¼" x 2¼" x ½" mortises to accept the runners. These mortises begin a ¼" from the end of the extension.

The runners are milled to size and a tenon is created on one end of each runner. I elected to notch the back edge of each runner so I could use a 1½" cut nail to hold the rear portion of the runner in place. The notch is ⅞" x 1¾". Add glue to the mortise-and-tenon, then add the nail to complete the installation of the runners.

Each runner needs a drawer guide. The guides are set square to the case front and flush with the face-frame edge.

Door Construction
The door is also constructed of ¾" stock, and it's the same mortise-and-tenon process and setup as was used on the face frame.

Once the door was glued, clamped square and the glue was dry, we fit it to the door opening in the frame using a nickel to gauge the offset on all four sides, and took passes at the jointer (one for one on each side) until the fit was perfect.

And here's Glen's hint to avoid tear-out along the top or bottom of the door frame: Because you'll be taking jointer passes off the end grain of the stiles, there's a very good chance that you'll splinter the outer edge of the stile. To avoid that, make a short cut from what will be the trailing end of the cut, then reverse the work and make the full cut. Because the material at the end is already gone, you won't have any tear-out.

Drawer Construction
I wanted inset drawers, which I was told (after the fact) are a little trickier to make than lipped drawers, because the fit has to be perfect or they won't look right. Because the fronts involved half-blind dovetails, we milled maple to ⅞" thick (you can go as thin as ¾", but the extra thickness provides a more antique look).

The drawers are graduated in size, from 4" - 6" in height, all are 15⅜" wide. (I just hope that bottom one will be deep enough to hold my hair dryer). First, we carefully examined the surfaced stock

to select the best faces for the drawers, then crosscut each front to length before ripping each front to width, making the fit very snug. We then pared each front to finished width, taking thin passes at the jointer on each edge until we had a penny-thickness offset on all four sides of each.

We milled the ½" drawer sides and backs out of poplar and cut them to

Cut the remaining waste on the tenon at the band saw, being careful not to overshoot your mark. If you do, the resulting kerf will show on the front of the door.

Here, the finished drawers are stacked and waiting for drawer bottoms and the finish.

To rout the rabbet for the glass, you'll be making some climb cuts. To avoid tearout, first make a shallow climb cut with the router, then go back and cut to full depth.

Use a 6" rule to extend the line of the rabbet, then clean the corner square with a chisel.

size; I then hand cut half-blind dovetails for the front, and through dovetails at the back.

After dry-fitting each drawer then knocking them apart, it was back to the table saw to cut a ¼"-wide x ¼"-deep groove ½" up from the bottom edge of each of the six side pieces, and on the three drawer fronts, for the drawer bottom. Add glue to your tails and pins, knock the drawers together and check for square, then set them aside to let them dry.

Next, mill poplar (or whatever secondary wood you choose) to ⅝" for the drawer bottoms, and cut them to size. What you're about to make is basically a country-style raised panel. At the table saw, set the fence to ³⁄₁₆", angle your blade to 12° and raise it so the blade exits cleanly through your workpiece.

Check the fit of the panels in your drawer grooves, mark a line where the inside edge of the drawer backs and the bottom panels meet. Pull the bottoms out and measure to find the center of each bottom and cut a saw slot set to the height of the line. Insert the bottoms into each drawer (you'll have an overhang at the back of ¼"), drill a pilot hole into the drawer back, then drive a cut nail through the slot in the drawer bottom, into the drawer back. This provides support for the bottom while allowing for seasonal movement. (In wider draw-

ers that require more support, space two slots across the back.) You could simply eschew the slot and nail straight through the drawer bottom, but the slot more easily accommodates seasonal movement in the drawer bottoms.

Back to the Door

Now we need to rout a ⅜" x ½" rabbet for the glass (or mirror, if you prefer) for the door. Set up your router with a rabbeting bit, set the depth to ½", then clamp your door face-down on your bench (you'll have to change the workpiece setup several times while routing the rabbet so you don't cut into your bench). Cutting the rabbet involves some climb cutting, so make sure you have a good grip on the router, and are holding it tightly and flat against your workpiece (a D-handle router makes this a little easier). To avoid ugly tear-out on the finish cut, first climb cut a shallow pass to waste out just some of the material. Then reverse directions (regular routing operation) and remove the rest, working your way around the interior of the door.

With the rabbet routed, you need to square the corners with a chisel. Press a rule against the inside of the rabbet, and extend the lines at each corner with a pencil to mark the area to be chiseled. First, make sure your chisel is sharp, then pare your way down ½" to the bottom of the existing rabbet.

Measure from side to side and top to bottom, and give your glass purveyor a call for both the panel glass and adjustable glass shelves. We ordered ¹⁄₁₆"-thick glass for the door, and ⅜"-thick glass for the shelves.

Now it's time to cut mortises for the hinges. While you could set up a router for this operation, with only two hinges to install, I opted for hand tools: two marking gauges, a chisel and mallet, and a small router plane to clean up the finished depth (which could be accomplished with a wide chisel, and a little more care).

Drill pilot holes for the hinge screws, and seat two screws in each hinge to make sure the fit is correct then transfer the hinge locations to the face frame, and remove the hinges from the door (you'll need them to mark around on the face frame). Cut your hinge mortises on the face frame, drill pilot holes for the screws, then install the hinges on the door. Hint: Put a smidge of paste wax on the screw, and it will seat more easily.

Now grab a buddy and have him or her hold the hinges in place on the frame as you install the door to ensure it fits. You'll then have to take it off and remove the hardware before finishing.

Building a Top Hat

The top frame and cove moulding completes the construction for the case. Mill

I cut the hinge mortises by hand using two marking gauges, a wide chisel and a router plane. If you don't have a router plane, use a chisel to pare the flat bottom.

To angle the drawer bottoms so they'll fit in the $5/8$" groove, you're basically making a raised panel on the table saw. Angle your blade to 12° and raise it so the angled blade exits cleanly through your workpiece.

the material to thickness and size according to the cut sheet.

The top frame houses another of our joints, the biscuit. The biscuit joint is used to join the two front mitered corners as well as the rear frame piece to the sides of the frame.

Cut the 45° miters at the miter saw, locate the center of the angled cut and use the plate joiner to create the slot for the biscuits. The wider rear frame has the slot centered on the ends with matching slots on the inside edge of the frame sides.

Assemble the rear frame to the sides with glue and biscuits, then clamp. Next, add glue into the remaining slots and assemble the frame. The trick to getting a square glue-up is to add another clamp across the front with one clamp along each side. Then, tighten the clamps so the mitered joints align.

Once the glue has dried, sand the

frame to #180-grit and profile the edges at the router table. We used the new Freud Quadra-Cut beading bit to profile the top frame.

Attach the frame to the case using #8 x 1¼" wood screws ensuring the frame is centered on the case and flush with the back.

The cove moulding is created with a raised panel bit at the router table. Use the full profile taking shallow passes until the top of the cove just touches the panel; there's no reveal.

Next, cut the mitered corners of the moulding, sand the profile smooth using #180-grit sandpaper and add the pieces to the case with 1" brads applied both to the case and into the top frame.

Backboards

I built a shiplapped back with three evenly spaced boards (a plywood panel would work, too). We ran two-step rabbets at the table saw, and I used a block plane to chamfer the edges that would show on the inside. Before installing the backboards, I painted the interior display area for some contrast with the clear finish on the outside, and to tie it in with the rest of the bathroom woodwork. Using the same template as for the side cutouts, we marked the back and made the cuts with a jigsaw.

Next, install a nailing strip at the bottom to which to attach the backboards.

The piece is screwed to the bottom of the bottom drawer runners with two #8 x 1¼" wood screws.

To install the backboards so that they'll accommodate seasonal movement, the idea is to use as few nails as possible. Two of the boards have only three nails: one at the top, one at the fixed shelf and one into a nailing strip at the bottom edge. The third board, because it has no lap to secure it flat, has two nails at either edge, in the same locations.

Finishing Touches

For the finish, we simply used a coat of sanding sealer and a coat of lacquer (sanding between coats) then wax.

Finally, you're ready to install the glass. It's held in the door with simple retaining strips pulled from the scrap bin and tacked in place with ½" headless pins (make sure you shoot the pins at an angle, wood to wood, so you don't hit and break your glass). Now install the catch for the door; we simply put it where we thought it looked good. For the final step, center the drawer pulls in each drawer, drill pilot holes then screw the pulls in place.

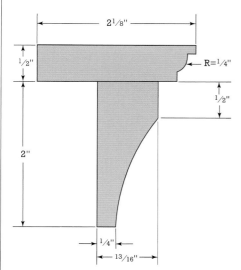

2⅛"

½"

R=¼"

½"

2"

¼"

13/16"

COVE MOULDING PROFILE

A Better Blanket Chest Design

BY CHRISTOPHER SCHWARZ

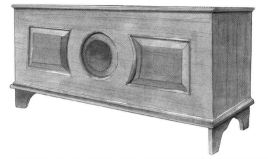

Three common forms of chests that show different strategies for the base.

Illustrations by Hayes Shaney

Though the chest is one of the oldest forms of furniture, that doesn't mean that the human race has settled on the best way to build it.

There are, in fact, many ways to build chests that make the process fussy, challenging and time-consuming – and the results look identical to a simpler chest.

To find the best way to build a chest, we surveyed plans and historical photographs of hundreds of examples from 1600 to the present. And then we boiled all that down to find the simplest way to build the complex chest shown here, which is an adaptation of a blanket box from the Shaker's Union Village community.

This may not actually look like a complex chest. But compared to historical examples, this chest was fancy in many ways. To understand why, let's look at the development of the form.

Community Chests

The first chests had all the joinery you'd find in a dugout canoe (that is, none at all). Early chests were made from one block of wood hollowed out with tools, fire or other forms of gumption.

Later, when riven boards became common, chests were built with two ends that also served as feet (the grain of these ends ran vertical). Then the front and back were fastened to the ends. This grain ran horizontal.

There were some other common variations as well, including assemblies where the ends, front and back became frame-and-panel constructions – and the stiles ran to the floor. Another type of chest

was a simple box propped up on feet that were turned or were slabs of wood.

On all forms of chests, moulding typically appears as a transition point between the box and the base or the box and the lid.

From there it was a short hop to make the chests out of two separate assemblies: the box itself and the base, which we call the plinth.

How to join the box and the plinth is the focus of this story. It doesn't have to be difficult for the chest's maker, but it sure can be.

Two Trying Designs

Traveling down the more difficult design path when building a chest begins with one assumption: That the plinth is merely moulding and should be applied to the box as such.

Once you make this assumption, here's one difficult (and common) way to make a chest: You cut a moulding profile into the top edge of the plinth pieces, join the plinth pieces at the corners and wrap them around the box. If you use a miter joint at the corner, it's fussy to fit the plinth exactly to the box – errors are

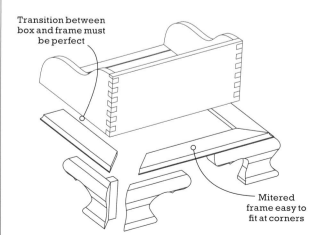

Transition between box and frame must be perfect

Mitered frame easy to fit at corners

PLINTH WITH BRACKET FEET

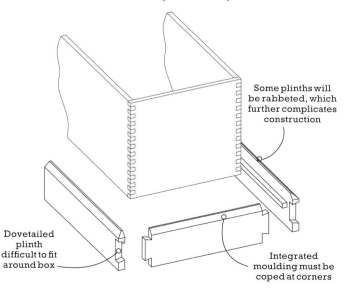

Some plinths will be rabbeted, which further complicates construction

Dovetailed plinth difficult to fit around box

Integrated moulding must be coped at corners

PLINTH WITH WRAP-AROUND MOULDING

When setting out all your joinery for the plinth (and the box above it), it's critical to mark your parts. I use a cabinetmaker's triangle to orient my front, back and end pieces.

easy to make and hard to hide. If you use dovetails, it is even fussier to wrap the plinth pieces because you'll have to cope the moulded edges at the corners.

Oh, one more thing – the plinth is like Atlas. It supports the whole chest, so you should use some fairly thick stock when making it, at least ¾" for a sizable chest. Or you need to add some glue blocks at the corners to support the box.

But what if you don't want that big ¾" step between the plinth and box? Well, you can cut a rabbet into the top edges of the plinth pieces, but then you are rabbeting, dovetailing and coping all your plinth pieces, and any error is going to result in a noticeable gap.

A variation of this particular design is supposed to make some of this easier. You wrap the plinth pieces around the box, and then you apply mitered moulding to the top edge of the plinth pieces. This hides any errors and makes the moulding easy to join at the corners.

And this does improve things. But it's still more work than necessary.

A second common way of building a plinth is to use bracket feet below a mitered frame that has its edge moulded. The mitered and moulded frame supports the box above. The bracket feet below support the frame. What's the downside? You need to get the fit between the box and the frame dead-on – or add another layer of moulding to hide any gap between the box and frame.

The above method is easier than

wrapping your moulding around the box, but we think there's an even better way to build this chest.

Detach Your Plinth

Though it seems counter-intuitive, it's easier to get a more accurate result with a chest like this if you build the plinth separate from the box so it acts as a platform for the box. Then you set the box on the plinth, drive a few fasteners and run moulding around the transition point to hide errors or irregularities.

Why is this better? For starters, you don't have to be as fussy with your joinery to make the outside dimension of your box match the inside dimension of your plinth. If your box or plinth end up a little bigger or smaller than intended, then you can size your moulding to accommodate the difference. It's a lot easier to trim ¹⁄₁₆" off a skinny piece of moulding than it is to remove that off the front and ends of a 16"-tall chest.

The other distinct advantage is that you don't have to jump through hoops if you want to use a delicate transition moulding. It's just as easy to make the transition large as it is small.

Plus, making the plinth separate doesn't require much more wood (it can be as little as two sticks). And the extra material is hidden so it can be an inexpensive or ugly species.

Finally, making a separate plinth allows for easier repairs, should that ever be necessary. You can easily detach the plinth or even replace it.

About the Union Village Chest

The Union Village Shaker community is near our offices in Cincinnati, Ohio, but it doesn't figure large in the world of Shaker furniture like the eastern Shaker communities do. Union Village was the first and largest Shaker community west of the Allegheny Mountains, and it was the parent community for the western Shaker communities in Ohio, Kentucky, Indiana and Georgia.

Founded in 1805, more than 4,000 Shakers lived at Union Village during its peak, selling herbal medicines, seeds and brooms. The community declined until it was sold in 1912, and the structures are now a retirement community.

One of the artifacts from the village

is a walnut blanket box with fine lines and tight dovetails. The box is similar to many Shaker chests that are extant, but this one has always been a favorite.

We chose to adapt this design because it highlights the advantages of our preferred chest-building method. The fine bit of transition moulding around the plinth is easy to accomplish with this construction technique.

While we retained the proportions and lines of the Union Village original, we used finger joints instead of dovetails. And we used figured maple instead of walnut. These alterations give the box a contemporary feel without looking like a pack of cigarettes with cabriole legs, or some such post-modern nonsense.

Begin the Building

Unless you possess wide boards (as the Union Village Shakers did), you need to glue up narrow boards into wider panels for the lid, front, back and ends of the box. The plinth and bottom are made from narrow stock. So while the glue in my panels was curing, I worked on the plinth.

The plinth has a front, back and ends that are joined with finger joints. Plus there are two "carcase supports" sunk into the plinth pieces. The carcase supports are housed in ⅜" x ½" rabbets that run the full length of the front and back, plus ⅜" x ½" stopped rabbets in the ends.

Cut the finger joints on the corners of the plinth pieces. After much experimentation, we found the best results came from plowing down the middle of the joint with a straight bit and then routing the sides. This eliminated the risk of our router shifting the parts around.

Once you get the corner joinery cut, plow the ⅜" x ½" rabbet on the top edge of the plinth's front and back pieces. Note that if you lay out your finger joints correctly, this rabbet runs through the entire length of the front and back pieces.

To cut this rabbet, I used a dado stack that was buried in an accessory wooden fence on our table saw. This method allows you to cut the joint with the work flat on the table, not on its edge.

Before you cut the curves on the plinth, assemble it. The corner joints will strengthen the feet as you cut the dramatic curve. To glue the joints, use a

Don't try to clamp your work in our finger-joint jig vertically. Gravity will fight you the entire time. Lay the jig flat and let gravity lend a hand as you position your pieces for routing.

When routing between the fingers, try to stay clear of the jig as you plow through the workpiece, as shown here. Then clean up the walls of the joint. This makes tighter joints.

Be sure to plan your plinth's finger joints so that the top of the front and back pieces can take a through-rabbet as shown.

slow-setting polyurethane or liquid hide glue. Yellow glue sets up too fast.

To clamp the finger joints, I made a bunch of small blocks of wood that I taped to the fingers. These little blocks allowed my clamps to put pressure right where it was needed.

After the glue has cured, remove the clamps, trim the end grain bits flush and make the ⅜" x ½" stopped rabbet in the ends of the assembled plinth. First cut a bunch of kerfs with a handsaw, then chisel the waste.

Then fit those carcase supports into the rabbets in the plinth. Glue and nail the carcase supports into the plinth's rabbets. Then get ready to cut the curves on the assembled plinth.

To cut the curves, first remove the bulk of the waste with a jigsaw, then clean up the curves with a plywood pattern and a router equipped with a pattern-cutting straight bit.

The curves on the ends, front and back are identical, so one short plywood pattern handles all the curves. To rout the straight run between all the curves, I clamped a straight piece of stock to the plinth and used that as a pattern.

Build the Box
The box above the plinth is fairly simple. Here's how it goes together: The corners are joined with finger joints. The bottom boards are shiplapped and nailed into rabbets in the front and back of the box. The till wall slides into a dado in the front and back. The till's bottom is nailed to cleats below.

The hinges are let into notches cut into both the back and the two hinge blocks, which are glued to the outside of the box's back. The hinge blocks support the hinge out to its barrel. And finally, the chest's lid is screwed to the hinges.

Begin by ensuring the front, back and ends of the carcase are indeed square. If they are out, you need to correct them before you rout the finger joints. Otherwise your carcase will go together all cockeyed. I prefer to shoot the ends of panels with a shooting board and a heavy plane. This is slower than making one mighty cut on the table saw, but it is unlikely to make things worse.

Cut your finger joints for the box. Then mill the ⅜" x ½" rabbet in the front and back pieces. Don't cut stopped rabbets in the ends – that's more trouble than it's worth. The dado stack set-up you used for the plinth's rabbets will do the same yeoman's job in the carcase.

Before you assemble the carcase, rout the ¼" x ½" x 6" dados for the till wall. This job is handled by a right-angle jig we developed for the router, shown in the photo below right.

Preparing for Assembly; Pulling the Trigger
Assembling finger-jointed carcases used to be one of the most stressful glue-ups in our shop. It usually involved every clamp in the shop, a helper and a bottle of Mylanta. That was back when we used yellow glue for the job. No more.

Yellow glue is probably the last glue you should use for this job. It sets up entirely too fast, leaving you with open joints and a sinking feeling in your stomach. Use polyurethane or liquid hide glue. If you are still unsure of your skills, use liquid hide glue, which is reversible with a little heat and water.

The two keys to a successful glue-up: A slow-setting glue and small plywood blocks that press the fingers together.

The easiest way to glue the corners together is to get them semi-assembled, then wipe glue on the long-grain surfaces inside the joint with a flat little scrap. Then apply the little blocks like you did with the plinth and turn on the clamping pressure. After the glue has cured, level all your joints and get ready to fit the interior parts.

Thinking Inside the Box

The bottom boards are shiplapped on their long edges, then nailed into the rabbets on the bottom of the carcase. Cut the shiplap rabbets on the table saw like you cut all the rabbets for the plinth and carcase. Cut the bottom boards to fit snugly, then space them out by inserting a couple quarters between each board. The 25-cent space allows the boards to swell during the wet months. Then nail the boards into the carcase's rabbets. No glue.

The till is simple. Fit the till wall into the dados in the front and back. Glue it in place. Then trim the till bottom to size. Glue and nail two till cleats below the bottom. Then nail the till bottom to its cleats. Again, rely on gravity and nails – not glue.

Carcase, Meet Plinth

Now you can join the plinth and carcase. Put the carcase upside down on the benchtop and center the plinth on the carcase. Screw the plinth to the carcase by driving through the carcase supports and into the bottom boards. About four screws in each carcase support will do the job.

Now you can figure out exactly how big your transitional moulding should be. Make your moulding (I used a ½"-radius cove bit and left a ¹⁄₁₆" fillet at each edge). Then miter it, tweak it, glue it and nail it.

A little alcohol and a block plane make light work of the proud end grain from the completed finger joints. The alcohol softens the tough end grain.

After you saw out the extents of the notch for the carcase supports, chisel the waste with some light chopping.

This is what you paid your money for when you bought this magazine: The two carcase supports hold the carcase in place and give you a place for your transition moulding.

Saw the curved shape of the plinth after assembly. If you do it before, the corners will be too fragile to clamp up without fussy cauls.

Normally, I would shape these curves with a rasp, but at the encouragement of our power-tool expert, I used a pattern-cutting bit and our trim router. I still like my rasps, but this is a very close second.

My shooting board and jack plane ensure that all my panels are dead square. These needed tweaking even after a ride on the sliding table on our table saw.

Shape the hinge blocks, attach them to the back of the carcase and then cut the recesses for the iron hinges. Screw the hinges to the carcase and then clean up your top piece for the last important detail.

Shaping the edges of a lid is something I always enjoy doing by hand with a plane. First shape the ends (which will blow out the long edges). Then shape the long edges to clean up the previous step's mess.

To shape the edges, I first mark the curve using a quarter, then I worked to that line with a traditional hollow moulding plane. A block plane will do the job, but it will leave a faceted surface that you should fair with hand sanding.

Then it's just a simple matter of screwing the lid to the hinges and adding some sort of stay to keep the lid propped open.

The router dado jig from *Woodworking Magazine* Spring 2005, Issue 3, is a favorite in our shop. (Any jig that lasts more than a few weeks in our shop is to be admired.)

Union Village Blanket Chest

NO.	ITEM	DIMENSIONS (INCHES)			MATERIAL	COMMENTS
		T	W	L		
Carcase						
1	Top	3/4	18	39	Maple	Edges radiused by hand
2	Front & back	3/4	15⅝	37½*	Maple	3/8" x 1/2" rabbet, bottom edge
2	Ends	3/4	15⅝	17¼*	Maple	
2	Hinge blocks	3/4	3	6	Maple	1/2" x 1/2" chamfer, one end
	Case bottom	1/2	36	16½	Poplar	Several shiplapped boards
1	Till wall	1/2	6½	16¼	Poplar	In 1/4" x 1/2" x 6½" dados
1	Till bottom	1/2	8	15¾	Poplar	Nailed to till cleats below
2	Till cleats	3/4	3/4	7	Poplar	Nailed to front & back
Plinth						
2	Front & back	3/4	5	38½*	Maple	3/8" x 1/2" rabbet, top edge
2	Ends	3/4	5	18¼*	Maple	3/8" x 1/2" notches, top edge
2	Carcase supports	1/2	3	37¾	Poplar	Fit in rabbets & notches
	Cove moulding	1/2	1/2	130	Maple	1/2" r. cove, nailed to plinth

* Cut these parts slightly longer and trim to final length after assembly

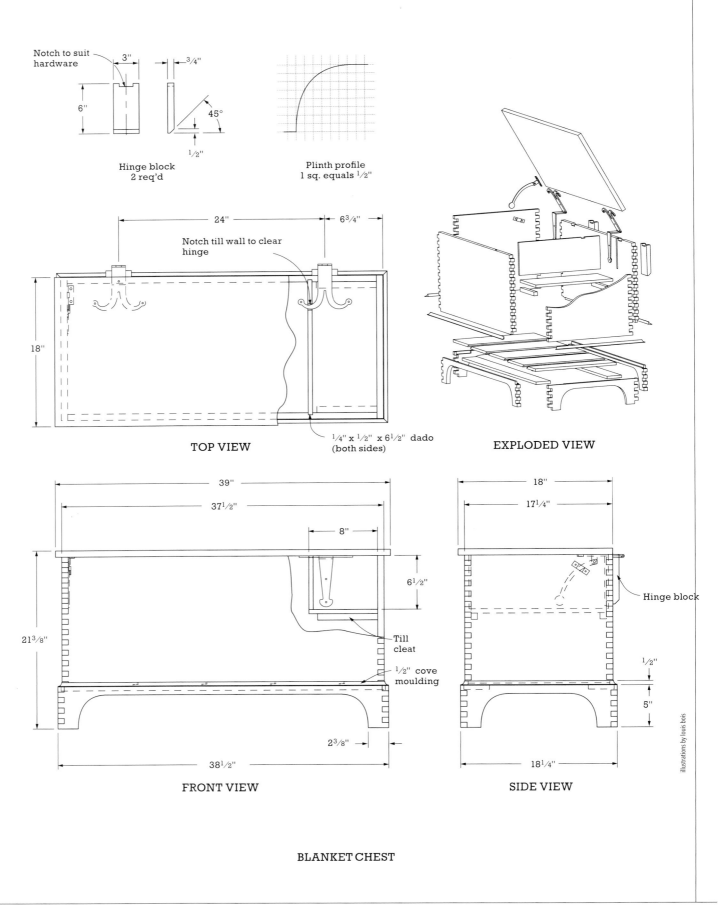

Notch to suit hardware

3"

3/4"

6"

45°

1/2"

Hinge block
2 req'd

Plinth profile
1 sq. equals 1/2"

24"

6 3/4"

Notch till wall to clear hinge

18"

TOP VIEW

1/4" x 1/2" x 6 1/2" dado
(both sides)

EXPLODED VIEW

39"

37 1/2"

8"

6 1/2"

21 3/8"

Till
cleat

1/2" cove
moulding

2 3/8"

38 1/2"

FRONT VIEW

18"

17 1/4"

Hinge block

1/2"

5"

18 1/4"

SIDE VIEW

illustrations by louis bois

BLANKET CHEST

Here the corners are nearly fitted and I'm smearing an oh-so-thin layer of polyurethane glue into each joint.

Finishing

This blanket chest was built during the winter months, so I had to use a hand-applied finish instead of spraying it in my driveway.

I've built a fair number of chests during the last 15 years, from tool chests to toy chests to other blanket chests similar to this Union Village version. Each had its charms, but each also had its rough spots, especially when massaging the transition between the base and carcase.

Not so with this chest. The only real challenge will be to decide which room of the house it belongs in.

Clamp the corners and then across the corners to pull the carcase into square. One clamp squared the entire carcase. You might need a clamp on the bottom as well.

With just eight screws, you'll keep the bottom rigid, the carcase in place and have a delicate step for the transition moulding.

Supplies

Van Dyke's Restorers

800-558-1234 or vandykes.com

2 black iron chest hinges (#02018071, $16.60 each)

Lee Valley Tools

800-871-8158 or leevalley.com

1 pair 8⅝" steel stays (# 01A62.20, $31.40/pair)

2 pkgs. #7 x ¾" pyramid screws (pkg. of 10, #01X38.76, $2.30/pkg.)

Prices correct at time of publication.

Shaker Stepback

BY MEGAN FITZPATRICK

I have a love-hate relationship with my television. I love (too much, perhaps) to watch shows, but I hate having the TV out in the open as the focal point of my living room. But I also dislike most commercial entertainment centers, as I've a penchant for antique and antique-style furniture.

So, I flipped through a pile of books on Shaker furniture and auction-house catalogs to cull design ideas for a step-back cupboard that could be repurposed as a modern entertainment center that would not only allow me to hide a 32" flat-panel TV behind doors, but also house the cable box, DVD player and various stereo components. (Of course, if you want to use it in your dining room, just omit all the holes in the backboards for air flow and cord management.)

A Plethora of Panels

While this project is quite large, it's surprisingly easy to build – though it's an exercise in organization to keep all the parts straight. The upper face frame, lower carcase and all four doors are simple mortise-and-tenon joints, with panels floating in grooves in the doors and carcase sides.

The first step is to mill and glue up all the panels. Use your best stock for the door panels, as they'll show the most. And here's a tip I didn't know until after it was too late: Keep all your cathedrals facing in the same direction and your panels will be more pleasing to the eye.

For the four doors, you'll need six ⅝"-thick panels, two each of three sizes. You'll also need two ⅝"-thick panels for the lower carcase sides.

A classic furniture form revised for 21st-century entertainment.

I wanted to glue up all the panels at the same time – but I ran out of clamps and space. Above are the six door panels and two lower side panels.

The majority of joints in this project are mortise-and-tenon. Take the time to set the hollow-chisel mortiser to cut dead-on centered mortises, $1\frac{1}{4}$" deep – it will save you a lot of frustration and time later.

The full dado stack on our table saw is $^{13}/_{16}$" and the tenons are $1^{1}/_{4}$" long, so I made the first cut on each face with the workpiece tight to the fence, then slid it to the left for a second pass. The blades are raised just shy of $^{1}/_{4}$" so I was able to simply roll the end of each $^{3}/_{4}$" workpiece to cut the tenons with one setup.

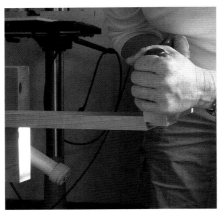

I purposely cut the tenons just a hair over-sized. I reached the final fit by testing each tenon in its mortise, then shaving each cheek as needed with a shoulder plane. And, I planed a slight chamfer on the tenon ends to make them easier to fit.

Unless you have access to a lot of wide stock, you'll also need to glue up ¾"-thick panels for the upper carcase sides, top, bottom and shelves, and the lower carcase bottom, shelf and top.

I glued up all my panels oversized. After the glue was dry, I took them out of the clamps, stickered them and set them aside. I cut each to its final dimension as it was needed, after calculating its exact measurement from the dry-fit frames and carcase sides. I don't trust cut lists; no matter how religiously I stick to the plan, measurements change in execution.

Mortises and Tenons Galore

With the panels set aside, I moved on to all the pieces that would be joined with mortise-and-tenon joints. Initially, I'd planned to concentrate on one carcase at a time to more easily keep things organized. I quickly realized that's an inefficient work method, as the mortise-and-tenon setups are the same on both the top and bottom pieces of the project. Rather than create each setup twice on the machines, I prepared all my stock and cut the joints at the same time.

First, chuck a ¼" chisel and bit in the mortiser, and take the time to make sure the chisel is dead parallel to the machine's fence. I began with the leg mortises – the only pieces on which the mortises aren't centered. After choosing the best faces for the show sides of each, mark which leg is which. Mark out

your mortises. On the inside back of the rear legs, they're set in 1" so the rail can accommodate the ⅝"-thick backboards. On the front and sides, they're ¼" back from the show faces, so that the rails end up flush with the front of the leg faces. The top rails are flush with the top of the legs, so lay out 1½" mortises on the inside front of the two front legs, and 2½" mortises on the side, ¼" down from the top. The bottom rails are all 3", so your mortises will be 2½", 1¼" up from the bottom of the leg.

Cut the mortises for the back rail first with 1" distance between the chisel and the fence, then change the setup to ¼" spacing, and cut the remaining mortises in the legs. To make clean mortise cuts, most of the Popular Woodworking editors use the "leap-frog method." That is, skip a space with every hole, then clean up between the holes. Some woodworkers prefer to overlap each hole to get a clean cut. Try both methods on scrap pieces, and use whichever you prefer.

Assuming your stile stock is exactly

¾" thick, the setup should remain the same for the face frame and door mortises, but double check that the chisel is centered in your stock before making that first frame cut. And, make sure you always work with the same side against the fence – if you are off a little bit, you'll be equally off on every joint, and cleanup will be easier.

Lay out all the mortises on your face frame and door frames and make the cuts. (A sturdy 6" rule is my preferred tool for cleaning the detritus out of the bottom of each mortise.)

Now it's on to the tenons. I prefer to set up the full 1³⁄₁₆"-wide dado stack at the table saw, and raise it to just shy of ¼". That way, I can make two passes on each end of my tenoned workpieces, and simply roll around each face to create the tenons, without having to change the setup at all for any of my 1¼"-long tenons.

With the tenons cut just a hair over-sized in thickness, I test-fit each one individually in its mortise and used a shoulder plane to reach the final fit. Planing

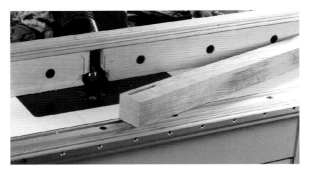

To cut $^3/_8$"-deep grooves for the floating panels, set up a $^1/_4$" three-wing cutter (also known as a slot cutter), using your mortises to set the cutter height. The groove will run from mortise to mortise.

Set up a fence-extension jig on the table saw, set the blade at a 12° angle, set the distance between the fence and blade at $^3/_{16}$" and raise the blade until it just clears the workpiece as the cut is made. This jig, built by Senior Editor Glen D. Huey, slides along the rail, so the workpiece can be clamped in place.

a slight chamfer at the end of the tenon will help it seat. (The fit should be a tight press fit. The tenon shouldn't move around in the mortise – nor should you need a mallet to get things together.)

Grooves for Floating Panels

With the mortise-and-tenon joints all dry-fit, it's time to cut the grooves that will accept the floating panels. Chuck a ¼" three-wing cutter into your router table, and raise it ¼" (you can use your already cut mortises to set the height – no measuring necessary). Set the fence to make a ⅜"-deep cut.

Start with the legs – and double check to make sure you have the faces marked correctly. The floating panels are on each side of the carcase, so a groove is needed from mortise to mortise on the front face of both back legs, and on the back face of both front legs. Unless your ear protection blocks out all noise, you should be able to hear the difference in sound as the router cutters move from the hollow of the mortise into the groove cut (mark the starting and stopping point if you're worried about recognizing the sound differential). With the leg flat to the table and the mortise toward the bottom, push the leg against the fence so that the router bit is spinning in the empty mortise hole, then move the leg across the table, cutting a groove that stops in the other mortise, then pull the leg away. Repeat until all four leg grooves are cut, and set the legs aside.

Test the bit height on your ¾" stock before proceeding. It shouldn't need adjustment … but it never hurts to be sure. Grooves are needed on all frame pieces that will house a panel – that's the inside edges of all the door rails and stiles, and on both long edges of the medial rails for the upper doors. On the stiles, the groove goes from mortise to mortise. On the rails, in order to cut a full ⅜" deep across the rail, you'll be nipping the inside edge of the tenon. That's OK – but be careful to cut away as little as possible so that the joint retains maximum strength.

Raised Panels

Now dry-fit the sides and doors and take the final measurements for all the panels. Add ⅝" to both the height and width of

each; with ⅜" hidden in the groove on all sides, you build in an ⅛" on either side for your panel. Retrieve the door and side panels from your stickered stack; cut them to final size at the table saw.

Now, set up a fence-extension jig on your saw – a stable flat panel attached to your rip fence will work, but that jig will be stationary and you'll have to carefully move your workpiece across the spinning blade. It's safer to make a jig that fits over the fence and slides along it. That way, you can clamp the workpiece to the jig and move the unit instead.

For any stock thickness, set the blade angle to 12°, and set the fence so there's ³⁄₁₆" between the fence and the inside saw tooth as the tooth clears the bottom of the throat plate. Raise the blade enough so that the stock fits between the blade and the fence (approximately 2¾"). This ensures the blade will clear the stock completely as the cut is made. Make sure you use a zero-clearance throat plate; otherwise, the thin offcuts will get caught and kick back.

Cut across the grain first, at the top and bottom edges. Any tear-out will be cut away on your second two cuts, which are with the grain. Clamp your workpiece firmly to the fence extension and slide it smoothly across the blade. Now repeat until all six panels are raised, and sand away the mill marks. These panels

will fit snug in the ⅜"-deep grooves, and allow for seasonal expansion and contraction. And if you prefer a more country look to a Shaker style? Face the raised panels to the outside of the piece and you're there.

Shapely Feet

At some point before you do any glue up, you'll want to turn your feet at the lathe and create a tenon at the end to join to the leg. (Of course, you could also add 6" to your leg length, and turn the foot on the leg stock. However, I decided I'd rather muck up a 6" length of wood than a 34" piece, so I made the feet as separate pieces.) I first milled each foot blank square, then turned them round and shaped each foot, following the pattern at right.

Even if each foot is slightly different (you can't tell unless they're right next to one another), be careful to turn the tenoned ends as close in size as possible. To achieve this, I set my calipers to ¾" and held them against the tenon as I cut the waste away with a wide parting tool. As soon as I reached a ¾" diameter, the calipers slid over the piece. I then turned the rest of the tenon to match.

Why make those tenons the same? Well, you have to fit the tenons into drilled holes that are centered in the bottom of each leg, and I wanted to use but

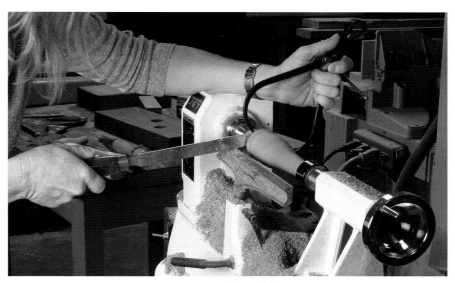

I shaped my 6" feet on the lathe and turned a ³⁄₄" x 1¹⁄₄" tenon at the top of each. While the feet needn't be identical, the tenons should be close in size. I held calipers set to ³⁄₄" against the piece as I used a parting tool to make the cut. When I reached ³⁄₄", the calipers slipped over the tenon and I was done.

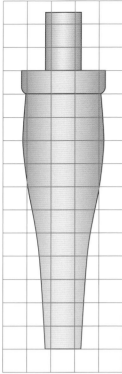

1 Square = ¹/₂"

FOOT LAYOUT

Before the bottom carcase is glued up, drill holes to receive the tenons on the turned feet. I used a ³/₄" Forstner bit to drill 1¹/₄"-deep. Match your bit and depth to the size of the tenons on your feet.

one drill bit and achieve a tight fit.

I clamped each leg perpendicular to the floor, and drilled ¾"-diameter x 1¼"-deep holes centered in the bottom of each leg. Be careful to keep your drill straight (or set up a drill press for greater accuracy). With the holes drilled, I set the feet aside until the rest of the bottom carcase was done.

Time for Glue Up

Dry-fit all your panels to the grooves inside the door frames and the bottom case sides, and make any necessary adjustments. Once everything fits snug, get your clamps ready and work with one glue-up at a time (I started with the lower doors and side panels, as they involved fewer pieces).

Use an acid brush to apply a thin layer of yellow glue on the walls of your mortises and the tenon faces, slip the rails in place, then slide the panel in place and cap it off with the opposite stile (keep a damp rag handy to wipe away any squeeze-out). Clamp until the glue is dry. (Again, add glue only to the mortise-and-tenon joints; the panels should float.)

The upper doors are a bit tricky to glue up, with two panels plus the medial rail in each. I'm sure my contortions were amusing to watch. I recommend getting a friend to help wrangle things in place.

While you're waiting for the lower sides to dry, glue up the upper face frame, check it for square, clamp and set it aside. Once the lower side panels are set, complete the lower carcase's mortise-and-tenon joints by gluing the lower back rail, the front rails and the center stile in place. (The upper back rail is notched around the legs at both ends, so it's easier to use pocket screws for that joint, though you can cut a mortise-and-tenon joint if you prefer.)

Now it's on to the upper section. Cut your sides, top, bottom and shelves to final size. The ¾"-thick top, bottom and shelves are housed in ¼"-deep grooves cut into the side pieces. So set up the dado stack again at the table saw but use only enough blades and chippers to create a ¾"-wide cut (and be sure to run a few test pieces first). Raise the stack to ¼". Mark the cuts on one of the case sides and set the fence off that piece, making

the cuts in both sides before moving the fence for the next location. Make sure your cuts are on the inside faces of your sides. Note in the illustration that the top and bottom pieces are not at the ends; they're set in to add rigidity, and the bottom protrudes ¼" above the face-frame bottom and thus functions as a door stop.

Before you take off the dado stack, run a ¾"-deep x ⁷/₁₆"-wide rabbet up the back of each side; these will house the backboards.

Now lay one side piece flat on your workbench (groove-side up) and fit the top, bottom and shelves into place. Set the other side piece on top, and use a dead-blow mallet to fully seat the pieces in the grooves. (This is a big workpiece – you might want to grab a helper.) If the pieces fit together snug, you could pull them back out, add a little glue and refit them. But after struggling to get them in place once, I didn't want to go through that exercise again (and it was a lot of exercise). Instead, I chose to toenail the shelves in place from the bottom face at both the front and back edges.

At this point, I also pegged all the mortise-and-tenon joints, and pegged the shelves in the upper carase into the sides, using ¼" white oak pegs (for more on pegging, see "Square Pegs, Round Holes" in the techniques section at popularwoodworking.com).

Now fit your doors to the face frame, and mark then cut the hinge mortises. Keep the door fit tight – you'll do the final fitting once the entire carcase is together (things could move when you add the backboards later – trust me). You might as well fit the lower doors and hinges at the same time.

Now, flip the upper carcase on its back and glue the face frame in place, adding enough clamps to pull it tight along each side. If things work out correctly, you'll have a slight overhang on both sides, which, after the glue dries, you can flush to the face frame with a trim router or handplane.

Backboards

Is that dado stack still in your table saw? Good. Mill enough ⁵/₈"-thick stock for your backboards for both the top and bottom, and run ⁵/₁₆" x ⅜" rabbets on opposing edges for shiplaps (and don't forget to calculate the rabbets as you're measuring the width of your rough stock). The outside pieces get only one rabbet each.

I used random-width boards pulled from an old stash of sappy cherry. Because the backboards will be on view with the doors open as I watch TV, I didn't want to use a less attractive secondary wood. So I used less-attractive pieces of primary wood. With the rabbets cut, change the table saw set-up back to a rip blade, and rip the outside backboards to final width (the humidity was low here when I built this, so I used dimes as spacers).

Screw the backboards in place, with one screw at the top and bottom of every board set just off the overlapping edge. (That screw holds the joint tight, but allows for slight movement of the underlapped piece. Your last board needs two screws at the top and bottom to keep it secure.) Now do the final fit on your doors, taking passes with a handplane or on the jointer (take a 1" cut on the trailing end first, then reverse the piece to avoid tear-out). I aimed for a ¹⁄₁₆" gap all around (on some sides, I even hit it). After marking locations for any necessary wire and air-circulation holes in the backboards, take the doors and backboards off, drill any needed holes at the drill press, then set the doors and backboards aside for finishing. Drill any cord/air holes at the drill press with a Forstner bit.

Complete the Bottom
Flip the lower carcase and choose your foot position. Line up the grain of the foot with its matching leg so the look is pleasing. One of my holes was a bit off straight, so I used a rasp to take down one side of my tenon until I could adjust the angle accordingly. Once everything fits to your satisfaction, drip a little yellow glue in the holes and seat the feet. You don't need clamps here (unless you're using them to pull something in line). If the fits are good, simply flip the piece upright and the weight will keep the feet in place as the glue dries.

With the backboards and doors off, now's the time to fit the cleats that support the bottom and shelf in the lower section, and cut button slots in the top

rail to attach the top. The bottom is notched around the legs and the back edge is rabbeted to fit neatly over the back rail. But because I need airflow in the bottom section for A/V equipment, I fit the shelf to the inside corner of each leg and to the front center stile where it serves as a door stop. I left a gap at the back and sides to run wires and for air circulation.

To complete the bottom section, use a biscuit cutter to cut slots in the front and side rails for buttons, and notch the upper back rail around the rear legs and use pocket screws to hold it in place. For added strength, countersink a screw through the front edge at each end into the leg, too. Cut the top to final size, and attach it with buttons at the front and sides. Countersink screws underneath through the back rail into the bottom of the lower section.

The Crowning Touches
Set up your table saw to cut crown moulding, and sand it smooth before fitting.

Often, the crown is connected with a flat piece to the top edge of the sides and face frame. But my face frame and sides weren't high enough, so instead, I cut blocks with 45° angles (on two faces for the corner pieces), glued those to the inside of the crown and added brads to the top of the carcase for a bit of additional strength.

The Finish
I sanded each piece to #180 as I went along, so once the construction was complete, I was ready for the finish. Because I didn't have two decades to wait for a nice warm patina to develop (we shot the opening picture just 20 minutes after the handles were in place), I added warmth

The top of the bottom section is attached to the side and front rails with buttons. I used a biscuit joiner to cut two ¹⁄₂"-deep x 1¹⁄₄"-wide slots on each side, and three along the front. I simply screwed through the back rail into the top's bottom to secure it at the back.

The crown is cut by running ⁷⁄₈" x 4" stock at an angle over the table saw. Raise the blade to ⁷⁄₁₆" then center your stock to the blade. Clamp a long straightedge to the table to guide the stock, then lower the blade and make a series of passes as you gradually raise the blade until you reach ⁷⁄₁₆" (or your desired depth).

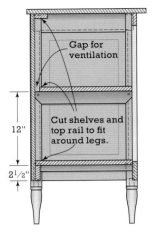

BOTTOM CASE SECTION

Gap for ventilation

Cut shelves and top rail to fit around legs.

12"

2$\frac{1}{2}$"

I intended for the top of the carcase to match the top of the crown, so I could attach the crown with a piece that tied into both. That didn't happen. So instead, I cut blocks with a 45° angle on the front, and glued them to the top of the carcase and the inside face of the crown — one at each front and back corner and three more along the front. You can also see the shiplapped back in this picture. Each piece is secured top and bottom at the corner by a screw.

3/4"

8$\frac{3}{4}$"

11"

27$\frac{3}{4}$"

1$\frac{1}{2}$"

BACK ELEVATION DETAIL

15$\frac{1}{2}$"

1/2"

1$\frac{1}{2}$"

13$\frac{5}{8}$"

16$\frac{5}{8}$"

PROFILE

49$\frac{1}{4}$"

2" reveal on top rail

1$\frac{1}{2}$"

54"

88$\frac{3}{4}$"

34$\frac{3}{4}$"

40$\frac{1}{2}$"

44"

ELEVATION

with two sprayed coats of amber shellac and a top coat of dull-rubbed-effect, pre-catalyzed lacquer.

Because I couldn't afford five sets of hand-forged iron hinges but wanted an aged look to the hardware, I de-lacquered then added patina to brass hinges with gun bluing.

Oh yes – the handles. I tried to turn them, but ran out of time and talent. Thank goodness for our local wood-working store and its Shaker pull supply. The handles were sprayed separately, set in a scrap of plywood. You see, I didn't know where I wanted to place them until the entire piece was assembled and the A/V components were in place. A friend helped me hoist the upper piece atop the lower cabinet, where it's held in place simply by gravity. I then marked my pull locations, drilled ⅜" holes with a Forstner bit and glued the pulls in place.

Supplies

Lee Valley

800-267-8735 or leevalley.com

4 pr. 3" x 1^{11}/₁₆" narrow extrude brass fixed-pin butt hinges (#00D02.04, $21.70 per pair)

Rockler

800-279-4441 or rockler.com

4 1⅛" cherry Shaker pegs (#78469, $9.99 per pair)

Prices correct at time of publication.

Shaker Stepback

NO.	ITEM	DIMENSIONS (INCHES)			MATERIAL	COMMENTS
		T	W	L		
Upper Section						
2	Face frame stiles	¾	1¾	52¾	Cherry	
1	Upper face frame rail	¾	3½	43	Cherry	TBE*
1	Lower face frame rail	¾	2	43	Cherry	TBE*
2	Side panels	¾	12	52¾	Cherry	
1	Top	¾	11⅜	43	Cherry	
1	Bottom	¾	11⅜	43	Cherry	
2	Shelves	¾	11⅜	43	Cherry	
4	Door stiles	¾	2½	47¼	Cherry	
2	Door top rails	¾	2½	17¾	Cherry	TBE*
2	Door center rails	¾	2	17¾	Cherry	TBE*
2	Door bottom rails	¾	2½	17¾	Cherry	TBE*
2	Upper door panels	⅝	15⅞	17¾	Cherry	
2	Lower door panels	⅝	15⅞	22¾	Cherry	
1	Front crown	⅞	4	49½	Cherry	Trim to fit
2	Side crown	⅞	4	15¾	Cherry	Trim to fit
Varies	Backboards	⅝	varies	52¾	Cherry	
Lower Section						
4	Feet	1¾	1¾	7¼	Cherry	1¼" dowel at top
4	Legs	1¾	1¾	28	Cherry	
2	Side panels	⅝	13⅞	21⅝	Cherry	
4	Side rails	¾	3	15¾	Cherry	TBE*
1	Upper front rail	¾	2	43	Cherry	TBE*
1	Lower front rail	¾	3	43	Cherry	TBE*
1	Upper back rail	¾	2	42½	Poplar	
1	Lower back rail	¾	2½	43	Poplar	TBE*
1	Center stile	¾	2	24½	Cherry	TBE*
2	Door panels	⅝	14⅞	17⅝	Cherry	
4	Door stiles	¾	2½	22	Cherry	
4	Door rails	¾	2½	16¾	Cherry	TBE*
2	Middle shelf cleats	¾	15½	2	Cherry	
2	Bottom shelf cleats	¾	14½	1	Cherry	
1	Top	¾	18¾	47	Cherry	
1	Shelf	¾	14½	42½	Cherry	
1	Bottom	¾	15¼	42½	Cherry	
Varies	Backboards	⅝	random	27	Cherry	

* TBE=Tenon both ends, 1¼"

William & Mary Chest

BY CHUCK BENDER

Early in my career I met an avid antiques collector whose focus was objects from the William & Mary period. Like many people, my first reaction was, "That stuff with those big, ugly ball feet?" Under his guidance I began studying various periods of furniture and their corresponding decorative and fine arts. Learning about the furniture, metalware, paintings and other decorative objects from the periods surrounding William & Mary helped me to understand how crucial and pivotal this period is to furniture design and construction.

The more I looked at Pilgrim, Queen Anne and Chippendale furniture, the more I began to like the sheer simplicity of the William & Mary designs, including those "big, ugly ball feet." After looking at countless examples, I no longer consider them big or ugly, and have come to appreciate the variety of designs.

The best thing about making a William & Mary chest of drawers is that it provides great skill-building exercises for the novice woodworker, yet enough challenge for an experienced builder. Whether you make ball feet (sometimes referred to as bun feet) is entirely up to you. This chest looks just as good with bracket feet as it does with bun feet.

The carcase is made up of two end frames with flat, floating panels that are joined with a few structural members. Once the case is together there are applied mouldings that dress it up. The dovetailed drawers are supported using an early method – side-hung drawer runners. You may not have tried this technique before, but give it a whirl – you may come to like it more than other traditional methods.

Lay it Out

Even with a detailed computer model, the first thing I do when building any piece of furniture is make a layout stick. It helps me mentally build the piece before I've even selected the lumber. With a layout stick I can work out joinery problems before they become real, and I can double-check all my sizes because I'm drawing everything at full size. Plus, it helps identify the areas where I might need to pay particular attention.

In case you've never heard of a layout

Using a full-sized sectional layout helps you avoid errors and visualize potential construction problems.

Put as much detail on your layouts as you need, but keep it understandable. I use different colors for each of the three views (below).

stick, it's a simple sectional, full-sized mechanical drawing of each of the three views of a piece: height, width and depth. Occasionally, I'll do special detail layouts as well, but for this project a three-section view is more than sufficient.

Another great reason to use a layout stick is that once you've double-checked all your measurements, you won't need to use a tape or rule again during the construction process. Every time you measure, you introduce opportunities to cut things to the wrong dimensions.

Begin with a scrap of wood that exceeds the longest measurement on the chest, but is only as wide as necessary to draw the detail of a large part, in this case the width of a stile.

I begin with the height view by drawing a line that represents the floor, then I measure up and mark the overall height (here, that's 38¾"). Measure down the thickness of the top and put a mark then do the same for the foot height, mouldings and all of the drawer blades.

I also like to detail my layout sticks with moulding profiles and other pertinent details (parts that are hidden from view are represented by dashed lines).

It's best if you make your layout stick as detailed as possible – without making it confusing. Sometimes, if you try to include every detail, the sheer number of lines can become so overwhelming that you render the layout stick useless. A good rule is to include each detail on at least one view; everything doesn't need to be on all three. After the height layout is finished, I move to the width and depth layouts.

Figure it Out

My next consideration with any project is wood selection. This is particularly important when building anything with frame-and-panel construction. I like to use straight-grained or quartersawn material for the stiles and rails to visually outline highly figured panels – but that's not where the process ends.

Take the time to carefully lay out your materials to obtain optimal use of figured woods. Sometimes this means removing usable material to get the best match.

Consider the visual balance of the individual pieces as well as how they will be part of a whole. I like to orient figure to give the piece a sense of symmetry and to draw the eye to various features.

This concept is particularly important when it comes to drawer fronts. If, for example, you're using curly or striped material, you don't want all the stripes angled in one direction because that would make your piece look as though it leans to one side.

While you can use highly figured material throughout an entire piece, that tends to visually homogenize the wood rather than accentuate the grain. When composing with wood, it's worth taking the time to get your materials properly laid out before you start building.

Frame it Up

With your lumber milled to rough size, the best place to start is to make the frames for the case ends. Working directly off the layout stick, you can quickly and easily mark all your parts to final dimension. Joint the edge of your stiles and rails then take them right to the layout stick; if you line up the jointed edge with the appropriate mark on the layout stick, you can directly mark the width of the pieces. At the table saw, rip them appropriately.

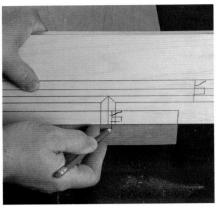

Transferring dimensions directly from the layout stick to the material reduces the potential for miscuts.

Sometimes the materials just don't cooperate. In this case, the lumber for the bottom rails wasn't wide enough. I scabbed on one strip that will be covered by the base moulding at the glue line, and another for the sticking, in which the seam will fall at the fillet.

Use a chisel to clean up the shoulder after you've cut the haunch.

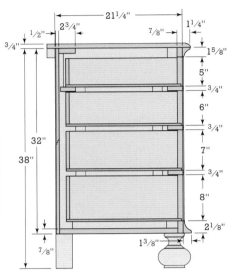

SECTION

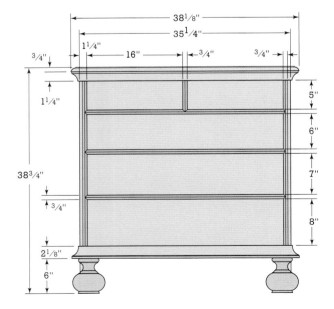

FRONT

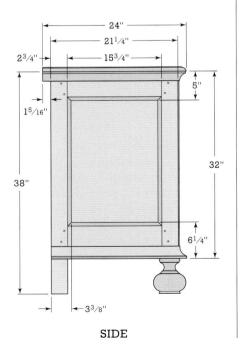

SIDE

You'll get a cleaner cut off the router bit if you rabbet and chamfer the workpiece prior to running the profile on the stiles and rails.

Using a round-nose router bit to make the concave portion of the cyma recta moulding allows you to get the proper shape without specialized tooling.

Use the rip fence as a stop to make accurate miter cuts a breeze. (Use the miter gauge to guide the workpiece.)

To cut them to length, square one end and use the layout stick to transfer the final length before you cut. Whether you're working with power tools or only hand tools, having a single benchmark (your layout stick) from which to mark multiple parts increases your accuracy.

Now that the stiles and rails are cut to size, I "stick" the edges of the pieces. ("Sticking" is the term used for running a moulded edge.) There are a couple of ways this can be done; I prefer a router.

This chest has a cyma recta moulding along the edge of the stiles and rails. Most commercial router bits are too exaggerated to provide the proper look. But if you think of your router as a motorized version of a set of hollows and rounds, the moulding is easy to make.

Begin by sketching the profile onto the end of a scrap that's milled to the same thickness as the stiles and rails. If you're not good at drawing, use tracing paper and copy the profile from the drawings provided (on page 117). Whether you are using hollows and rounds or a router, you can benefit from cutting rabbets and chamfers to remove the bulk of the waste. This step helps ensure more uniform mouldings throughout.

William & Mary Chest

NO.	ITEM	DIMENSIONS (INCHES)			MATERIAL	COMMENTS
		T	W	L		
2	Front stiles	$1^1/_4$	$3^3/_8$	32	Cherry	
2	Back stiles	$1^1/_4$	$3^3/_8$	38	Cherry	
2	Top rails	$1^1/_4$	5	$19^3/_4$	Cherry	2" TBE*
2	Bottom rails	$1^1/_4$	$6^1/_4$	$19^3/_4$	Cherry	2" TBE
2	Panels	$3/_4$	$15^3/_4$	22	Cherry	
1	Case bottom	$7/_8$	$19^3/_4$	34	Poplar	
1	Top front rail	$7/_8$	$1^5/_8$	$34^1/_4$	Cherry	$3/_4$" TBE
1	Bottom front rail	$7/_8$	$2^1/_8$	$34^1/_4$	Cherry	$3/_4$" TBE
3	Drawer blades	$3/_4$	$2^1/_2$	$34^1/_4$	Cherry	$3/_4$" TBE
1	Back drawer blade	$3/_4$	$2^1/_2$	$34^1/_4$	Cherry	$3/_4$" TBE
1	Drawer divider	$3/_4$	$2^1/_2$	$6^1/_2$	Cherry	$3/_4$" TBE
1	Back cleat	$7/_8$	$2^3/_4$	$35^1/_4$	Poplar	$1^1/_4$" DBE**
1	Runner support	$3/_4$	6	$17^3/_8$	Poplar	
1	Top	$3/_4$	24	$38^1/_8$	Cherry	$1^5/_{16}$" back overhang
2	Cove mouldings	$1^3/_8$	$2^1/_8$	96	Cherry	Base mould cut down
6	Double-arch mould	$3/_{16}$	$3/_4$	36	Cherry	Cut to fit
2	Drawer fronts	$7/_8$	5	16	Cherry	
1	Drawer front	$7/_8$	6	$32^3/_4$	Cherry	
1	Drawer front	$7/_8$	7	$32^3/_4$	Cherry	
1	Drawer front	$7/_8$	8	$32^3/_4$	Cherry	
10	Drawer runners	$1/_4$	8	$19^1/_4$	Oak	Nailed to stiles
1	Back	$1/_2$	32	34	Poplar	Multiple pieces
2	Foot dowels	$7/_8$	$7/_8$	$6^7/_8$	White oak	
2	Feet	$5^1/_2$	$5^1/_2$	6	Cherry	Glued up

*TBE = Tenon both ends **DBE = Dovetail both ends

Using an appropriate core-box or round-nose router bit, run the hollow portion of the cyma curve. To cut the convex or round portion of the curve, I find a shoulder plane easier to use to achieve the shallow arc than using a commercial router bit – a No. 6 hollow plane does the trick nicely as well.

After running the sticking, head to the table saw and use a dado stack to run a ⅜"-wide x ⅝"-deep groove for the panel in all eight frame pieces. The groove does several things; most importantly, it gives me a place to align my mortises, and it serves as a haunch on the inside edge of the frame parts.

The top rail tenons are haunched 1" off the outside edge; the bottom rails are haunched at 1¾". With the mortises laid out on the stiles, grab your favorite ⅜" mortise chisel (mine fits into a hollow-chisel mortiser) and chop them. Once you're set up, it makes sense to cut all your mortises at the same time. So use your layout stick to mark the mortise locations on the stiles for the drawer blade and the vertical drawer divider mortises, then cut them, too.

Now cut the drawers blades and center divider to final dimensions before moving onto the tenons – as with the mortises, it's more efficient to cut those in one session.

I use a dado stack to make my tenons. It's quick and cuts the cheeks and shoulders in one motion. After cutting the tenons, the miter cuts (that allow the stuck moulding to meet nicely in the corners) need to be marked. Forego using the layout stick for this. At several points in any build, using the layout stick becomes counter-productive. The layout is theoretical; the real parts give you actual dimensions. Always go with the actual dimensions when you can. I align the stiles and rails, then transfer the miter locations directly from one frame member to another.

Tilt the table saw blade to 45° and, using the rip fence as a stop (one position for the rail cuts and a second for the stile cuts), cut the miters. Set the stop to leave the miters a little heavy. They are easily adjusted by passing a handsaw through the assembled miter to remove minute bits of excess material until the tenon shoulders and miters come together.

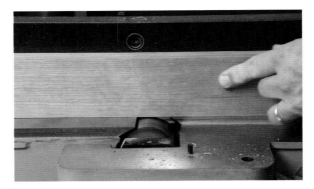

At the jointer, a single pass to remove the sticking waste is fast and accurate.

After jointing off the waste, use a sharp chisel to pare the shoulder to the miter.

With the frame dry-assembled, it's easy to transfer the location of the peg holes to the tenons.

At the drill press, offset the tenon's peg hole about ¹⁄₃₂" toward the shoulder to drawbore the joint tight.

With the miters cut on the frame moulding, you still need to remove excess sticking material from the stiles. My preferred method is to use the jointer. I set the depth of cut to match the width of the sticking (on some frames this could be considerable, so be careful when using the machine). In one deep pass, I remove the waste, stopping just short of the cutline. Then I clamp the stile in a vise and pare away the remaining waste.

Dry-fit the frames and cut the panels to size, using the actual frames for the dimensions, not the layout stick. Then bevel the inside face so the panel fits into the stile-and-rail grooves. Now it's time to prepare for assembly.

Begin by marking the peg locations

on the stiles (see the drawing at right). Drill ⁵⁄₁₆" holes for the pegs at the drill press. Dry-fit the mortise-and-tenon joints, making sure to transfer the peg-hole locations onto the tenon cheeks. Disassemble the frames to drill the same size holes in the tenons. Offset the holes about ¹⁄₃₂" toward the shoulder to take advantage of drawboring the joint.

You'll need to make some pegs out of straight-grained cherry. Rip the stock to ⁵⁄₁₆" x ⁵⁄₁₆" and cut pegs that are slightly longer than the thickness of the frame parts (about ¼" longer should do). Use a chisel to sharpen the pegs to a blunt point (a pencil sharpener also works well for this).

With the joints ready to go, I use

Transfer the inside lines from the stiles, then trim the waste on the band saw on all the double tenons. They will most likely need paring to fit perfectly.

Using an edge-routing jig to make dados and rabbets just means lining the jig up with the layout line then routing to the proper depth. It also makes cutting the stop rabbets for the backboards easy.

The poplar drawer-runner support is notched around the back cleat and drawer divider, then just nailed into place.

a cabinet scraper to remove all the machine marks on the interior and exterior surfaces. After I have all the parts of the frames scraped, I sand the outside faces of the panel and frame, as well as the sticking. Slather up the mortises and tenons with your favorite glue and assemble the frames. Lock the joints in place by driving the pegs home; a little beeswax on the peg sides helps them glide through the offset holes.

Get it Together

While the glue dries on the frames, mark out and cut the center waste on the three drawer blades' double tenons. Hold the drawer blades in place on the end assembly and transfer marks from the inner face of the mortises to the ends of the blades. These become the inner cheeks of the double tenons. I find it best to cut these on the band saw. A little paring with a chisel is usually needed for a proper fit.

Also fit the single tenons of the top and bottom front rails, and the double tenons on the drawer divider, which fits into both the top front rail and the drawer blade immediately below.

With the frame glue dry, level the

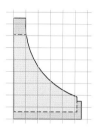

LOWER & UPPER CASE MOULDINGS
Grid = $1/4$" squares

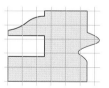

STICK MOULDING
Grid = $1/4$" squares

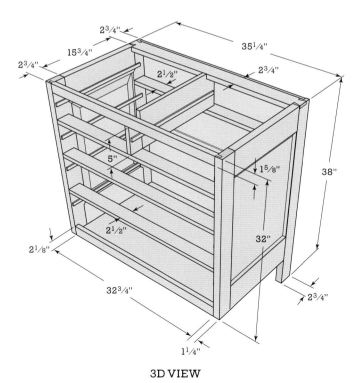

3D VIEW

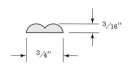

DOUBLE-ARCH MOULDING

mortise-and-tenon joints with a cabinet scraper, plane or sander. Set the frames inside up on a worksurface and lay out the ⅝" x ⅝" stop rabbets for the back-boards, and the ⅝" x ⅞" rabbet for the case bottom. I use an edge-routing jig and router with a straight bit to make these cuts.

The next step is to dovetail the back cleat into the top end of the rear stiles.

Dry-fit the entire case to determine the dimensions for the drawer runner support. (Its sole purpose is to hold the drawer runners on which the top two drawers slide.) In typical early 18th-century fashion, this support piece is notched around the drawer divider and top rear cleat. It's then nailed into place at the front and back after the case is glued-up. Prep all the case parts and glue up the carcase.

Dress it Up

While the glue dries on the carcase, all the case mouldings can be made. It's fairly common on early pieces to find upper and lower mouldings that use the same plane in different ways. For the upper and lower mouldings, I've used the same radius, but modified the overall size by making the lower moulding taller and deeper than the upper moulding by adding a ³⁄₃₂" step and a vertical flat (see the pattern at right).

Because the coves are made at the table saw, there is a single setup to make the foundation of both the upper and lower mouldings. Use tracing paper to draw the profiles on the ends of the blanks to help orient things properly. Position and attach an angled fence on the table saw, then run the blanks diagonally through the saw to create the coves. (For more on how to make cove moulding on the table saw, see the online extras.) Use the drawn profiles to set the saw to the various angles needed to complete both mouldings.

One quick tip: I like to prep (with a scraper, No. 18 round or sandpaper) the cove portion of the mouldings prior to making the angle cuts. This way the moulding blank lies flat on the bench and is easily gripped between a tail vise and bench dog.

The double-arch moulding can be made using a stock ⅜" bead cutter or

Thick stock isn't always available. "Packing out" the back side of mould-ings has been a practice in use for centuries. I've laminated a piece of poplar to each cherry moulding blank. The profile is trans-ferred from my layout stick to the end of the moulding.

I typically scrape, or plane and sand, the blank prior to finishing off the moulding. This way I don't inadver-tently obliterate additional elements of the moulding.

Hold the double-arch moulding in place to mark off the position of the drawer blades.

Once the location marks are in place, draw the miters to ensure a proper cut.

Cut the double-arch moulding miters on the band saw. Leave a little extra to be trimmed off before installation.

Make a 45° guide block to accurately trim the miters on the double-arch mouldings.

moulding planes. (You can use short sections of stock here; no need to stick a continuous 18' run.)

Run the double-arch mouldings on the edge of a wider blank; that makes it easier to hold the workpiece in a vise for sanding before you rip the moulding free.

Before attaching the upper and lower mouldings, cut the top to size and install it. Measure the dimensions of the carcase and add the appropriate overhang for the sides and front (1⁷⁄₁₆"), and the back (1⁵⁄₁₆"). Yes, I said back. Another fairly common practice on period furniture is to have the top overhang the back. When the piece is pushed against the wall, the top clears the baseboard and chair rail, preventing your stuff from being trapped between the chest and the wall.

After the top is cut to size, run an ovolo along the front edge and ends using a ½" roundover bit. There is about a ³⁄₃₂" flat at the top of the ovolo, which means the router bit falls short of the bottom edge. Sandpaper easily knocks off any residual line.

After the glue dries, level the joints (if needed) and remove any clamp damage to the case then attach the top. Simply align it properly and drill through the top into the stiles. The pegs on this chest are ⁵⁄₁₆" square. It's better to drill that size hole through the top and a slightly smaller hole into the framework. (I reduced the diameter by about ¹⁄₃₂" for this cherry. In pine I'd reduce it more.) This allows for the compression of the fibers in the peg as it passes through the top.

If the holes in the top and frames were exactly the same size, there's a chance that the pegs might not grip the stiles. If you want a removable top, this is the way to go, but I like mine permanently attached. Once the top is pegged in place, wrap the upper and lower mouldings on the carcase then fit the double-arch mouldings around the drawer openings.

The double-arch mouldings align to the inside of the chest sides and are flush with the drawer blades. The mouldings on the blades are mitered into the stile mouldings. The drawer-divider moulding is mitered into the drawer blade below. Attach these pieces with glue and pins.

Half-lapped and beaded backboards complete the case. But don't attach them

yet; you'll find the next steps easier without them in place.

Hang 'em Up
Unlike drawers where the runners are underneath (you're likely familiar with this type), side-hung drawers literally hang on a runner that mates with a groove on the drawer side. The runner is nailed to the inside of the case.

When planning joinery for side-hung drawers, the primary consideration is groove placement for the runners. The dovetails need to be laid out so that these grooves fall into a tail. This avoids having to remove end grain of a pin and allows the drawer front to act as a stop.

The grooves are ¼" deep x ¾" wide. I make the runners from ¼"-thick material that is about 2³⁄₃₂" wide.

The runners are nailed into the stiles of the case at the proper position. To find that location, I dry-assemble the drawers and place them into the openings. Working from the backside of the carcase, transfer a mark for the top of the groove to the case side. I bump the line up about ¹⁄₃₂" or so toward the top of the opening to ensure the drawer bottoms don't drag on the drawer blades. Use a large square to strike the line across the inside face of the case sides and the center divider.

With the locations marked, tack the runners in place using small brads. This allows you to test the position. Once the drawers are complete, make any adjustments then nail the runners. Rosehead nails were commonly used in period work to secure runners. If you go this route, be sure to drill countersink holes to allow the heads to be set flush.

The drawer construction is straightforward. The fronts are rabbeted and the bottoms are nailed to the bottom of the sides and back, and into the front rabbet.

And Now the Feet
Because the feet are of a large diameter, you may be-hard pressed to find stock of the appropriate size at your lumberyard. To achieve the proper diameter for these feet, I milled two faces of a 16/4 board flat and square. To these faces, I glued a flattened piece of 6/4 material with matching grain and color. This allows the foot to be turned the proper diameter while hiding

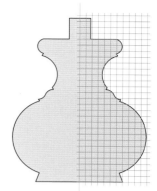

BUN FOOT
Grid = ¼" squares

Adding extra stock to the core material for the feet allows you to get a larger-diameter foot from readily available material. When complete, orient the glue lines so they are not apparent from the front of the chest.

Clamp the feet to get a grip on them while drilling. The peg holes go all the way through.

the glue joints as much as possible. Once the foot is turned, rotate the two patches to the inside and back of the foot. No one will notice your laminated feet.

The bun feet are attached with ⅞" oak dowels that extend through the foot and are glued into matching holes in the case bottom.

Wrap it Up

Before installing drawer bottoms and backboards, I color and finish the chest.

This does two things: It helps to avoid unsightly drips on the secondary woods, and it allows you to install the brasses without having the drawer bottom interfere. This is particularly important if you are using brasses attached with wires (or "snipes," as they are often called).

After your finish dries, all that remains is to install the hardware, and decide in which room you're going to display the fruits of your labor.

Supplies

Ball and Ball Hardware

ballandball.com or 800-257-3711

8 W&M A73 backplates with A69 drops (#A73-009)

3 W&M chased escutcheon (#L63-004)

Horton Brasses

horton-brasses.com or 800-754-9127

1 Wrought-head nails (#N-22, ¼ lb.)

Brush It Off

I'm often asked how I apply my finishes. While I'm not opposed to spraying, most of the time I find myself brushing. My finish of choice is shellac, so brushing is easy and quick.

Whether you color your pieces or go au naturel, you are going to need something to stop the wood from becoming soiled and damaged. That's what a top coat does – protect the wood. Many believe that brushing finishes is a skill that takes a lifetime to acquire. I believe, with a little practice and a few tips, you can be successful in short order.

To brush shellac you'll need a decent brush. I prefer a badger hair brush to other types. While they are not the cheapest brushes on the market, they aren't the most expensive, either (a 2" brush can be had for around $15). A good brush makes all the difference to me in how the final finish looks.

Regardless of whether you make your own shellac from flakes dissolved in alcohol or pour it out of a can, the key to getting a good finish is using it at the proper viscosity. More layers of thinner material are better than a few thick layers. Shellac's thickness is measured by how much is dissolved in the solution. A 3-pound cut, for example, is 3 pounds of flakes dissolved in 1 gallon of alcohol; a 2-pound cut consists of 2 pounds of flakes dissolved in 1 gallon of alcohol, and so on.

I usually start by putting on a washcoat (a.k.a. sealcoat) that is around a 1- to 1½-pound cut. The idea is to apply a thin coat of finish to seal the wood so additional coats build on top instead of soak in. The first coat will raise the grain of the wood regardless of how well you sanded prior. If you are worried about rubbing through the color as you sand between coats of shellac, you can raise the grain on the piece with water then lightly sand prior to coloring it. This reduces the amount of grain raising that takes place with the washcoat of shellac.

After the washcoat has dried, lightly sand with #280- to #400- grit "A" weight sandpaper. You can tack the surfaces clean or not. The dust left behind from sanding is primarily shellac that will re-dissolve as the next coat is applied.

Subsequent coats are applied at a thicker viscosity (I tend to use about a 2-pound cut). On this chest I ended up applying an additional five coats of shellac. If your shop is warm and dry, you can easily apply two or three coats per day without any trouble.

As I mentioned, I apply very thin coats. Regardless of the viscosity, I work with a relatively dry brush, dipping the tips of the bristles about ⅛" into the liquid then wiping them on the side of the container. The most important part of brushing shellac is to cover as much of the surface as quickly as you can. By keeping the entire surface wet with shellac you can use the tips of the bristles to flow out the finish and reduce brush marks.

When applying shellac to large, flat surfaces, begin brushing a few inches in from the edge and brush outward off the end of the board. Always brush along the length of the grain, not across it. Once you have the two ends of the surface brushed, you can flow everything in between without worry about runs or sags on the ends.

After the final coat is applied, my favorite way to complete the job is to rub out the surface with #0000 steel wool, mineral oil and pumice. Dab some oil onto a steel-wool pad then sprinkle a little pumice on it. Use your finger to knead the pumice into the oil-soaked steel wool, then lightly pass the pad across the finished surface. You'll need to frequently add oil and pumice to the pad until it becomes saturated. A light, deft hand will leave a silky-smooth finish.

Aumbry

BY CHRISTOPHER SCHWARZ

It is easy to forget that many of our favorite pieces of furniture are recent innovations. Forms such as coffee tables, bookcases and desks are – archaeologically speaking – new objects brought on by incredible modern wealth.

When you cast your eye back on the furniture record, the forms become simpler, fewer in number and (in some cases) quite unfamiliar. One of my favorite types of early furniture is the "aumbry" – sometimes called a dole or livery cupboard. It is the honored ancestor of the bookcase, hutch, cupboard, armoire and common kitchen cabinet.

Today the word "aumbry" is used to refer only to a liturgical piece of furniture or place in a church that holds the sacrament. But the word, and the piece of furniture, were both common and secular in the 1400s and 1500s. This enclosed cabinet held things that were precious – food, books, china and anything else that had to be locked up.

One of the defining features of aumbries is that the front of the cabinet is pierced by Gothic tracery. These piercings are not just decorative. They allow air to circulate inside the carcase, like a modern pie safe. To stop insects from getting inside the cabinet, the piercings were covered with cloth fastened to the inside of the case.

Aside from the pierced tracery, these cabinets are straightforward to build using simple tools and construction methods. Most aumbries are knocked together using basic joints – rabbets, dados and nails made from wood or iron.

This particular aumbry is based on a circa-1490 piece that was part of the Clive Sherwood collection sold at a Sotheby's auction in 2002. To make the piece more approachable, I simplified some of the tracery and removed some of the chip carving and knifework that festoons the front of the original. Despite these simplifications, this aumbry would look at home in any Medieval English or French homestead.

Start with the Oak

Most aumbries were made of oak. And because wide English oak is nearly impossible to get, I chose quartersawn American white oak for this aumbry. The original was made with planks that were

Clamp a batten on your layout line and saw the first wall of the dado. Press the sawplate against the batten to create a vertical cut.

Use the mating shelf to strike the second wall of the dado. Use a pencil or knife to mark this wall.

Because of the set of the saw's teeth, clamp the batten so it covers your layout line for the second wall. This will ensure your dado isn't too loose.

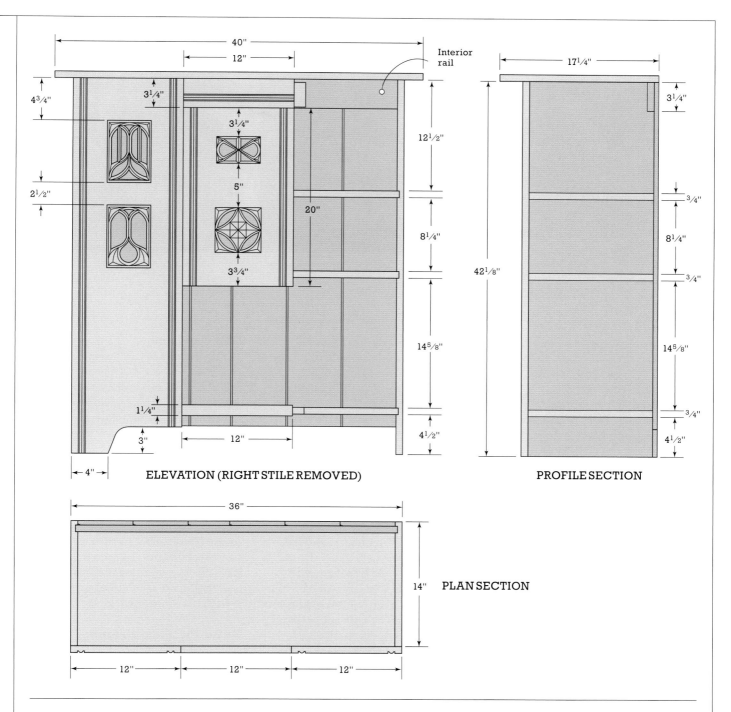

ELEVATION (RIGHT STILE REMOVED)

PROFILE SECTION

PLAN SECTION

American Gothic Aumbry

NO.	ITEM	DIMENSIONS (INCHES)			MATERIAL	COMMENTS
		T	W	L		
1	Top	$3/4$	$17^{1}/4$	40	Oak	
2	Sides	$3/4$	14	$42^{1}/8$	Oak	
2	Stiles	$3/4$	12	$42^{1}/8$	Oak	
1	Door	$3/4$	12	20	Oak	
1	Top rail	$3/4$	$3^{1}/4$	$14^{1}/2$	Oak	$1^{1}/4$" TBE*
1	Bottom rail	$3/4$	$1^{1}/4$	$14^{1}/2$	Oak	$1^{1}/4$" TBE*
1	Interior rail	$3/4$	$3^{1}/4$	35	Oak	
3	Shelves	$3/4$	$13^{1}/2$	35	Oak	
1	Back	$1/2$	$34^{1}/2$	39	Oak	Shiplapped

*TBE = Tenon both ends

Use wrought nails or rosehead cut nails to fasten the sides to the shelves. Use tape to remind yourself where the nails go – the tape is easier to remove than a pencil line.

The stopped groove for the interior rail is made the same way you made the dados for the shelves.

Drive the interior rail in place. Then fasten it from the outside of the case with two 6d rosehead nails at each end.

12" to 14" wide – a tall order these days. So I glued up the sides, top, stiles, shelves and door from two narrow pieces, taking care to match grain and color.

Because I built this aumbry almost entirely by hand, I took care to also make sure the grain direction in the panels was consistent. This detail makes life a lot easier for those who prepare wood for finishing with a handplane.

The case itself is as simple as it gets. The shelves are nailed into dados in the sides. The face frame, backboards and top are nailed to the carcase. The only complex bits are the mortise-and-tenon joints that hold the face frame's rails and stiles together.

And then there are the Gothic piercings. These are simple to make with a drill bit, a chisel and a couple of rasps. Don't be intimidated by them – they are easier than they look. To get started on your aumbry, glue up the panels for the entire case, then cut the two sides to their final size and get ready to cut the carcase joinery.

Handmade Dados

The ¼"-deep dados in the sides that hold the shelves are simple to make with a handsaw, chisel and a router plane. Begin by laying out one wall of each dado on the side pieces. Then clamp a scrap right on the layout line and use it as a fence for your saw. Saw down ¼" into the side to create the first wall of the dado. Do not remove the batten.

Place the mating shelf against the bat-

ten and use it to lay out the second wall of the dado. Reposition the scrap so it covers the pencil line, clamp it in place and saw the second wall of the dado on the waste side of the line.

Remove the majority of the waste with a chisel, then flatten the bottom of the dado with a router plane. Check the fit of the shelf. If the dado is too tight, rabbet the end of the shelf. If it's too loose, make some wedges to knock into the gap at assembly time.

Cut all the dados, fit all the shelves then prepare all these boards for finishing, inside and out. Assemble the case using hide glue and 6d rosehead cut nails. Cut nails were invented a few hundred years after the original aumbry was built, so they aren't authentic to the core. However, because blacksmith-made nails are expensive (about $1.50 to $2 apiece) and the roseheads look (fairly) authentic, I decided to use them.

A second option would be to fasten the sides to the shelves using glue and "trenails" or "trunnels," essentially tapered oaken nails.

A Rail for the Backboards

To make the carcase a bit sturdier, add an interior rail to the inside of the case. This rail, located at the back of the carcase, helps hold the backboards in place. To hold the interior rail in place, cut ¼"-deep stopped grooves for its ends. Make these stopped grooves just like you did your dados: Saw the walls, chop the waste and clean the floor with a router plane.

Add the Back

The back of this piece is assembled using several narrow boards. On many originals, the backboards were merely butted against one another and nailed on, as shown in the drawings. This works, but you will have ugly gaps there when the boards shrink.

To avoid that, cut shiplap joints or tongue-and-groove joints on the long edges of the backboards. I used shiplaps.

When attaching the backboards with nails, first use clamps to pull the carcase square. Then nail the backboards to the shelves and interior rail using 4d rosehead nails. The nailed-on backboards will hold the carcase square, making it easier to fit the face frame and the door.

Build the Face Frame

The pieces that adorn the front of the aumbry are much like a modern face frame. The wide stiles join the narrow rails with mortise-and-tenon joints. I chopped the ¼"-wide x 1¼"-deep mortises first, then sawed the tenons to match.

With the joints fit, you can cut the "crease moulding" that runs parallel to the long edges of the stiles and top rail. This is easy to make with simple tools. The crease moulding begins ¾" from the long edge of the board and is ¾"wide.

To begin, plow ⅛"-wide x ³⁄₁₆"-deep grooves on either side of where the moulding is located. Then shape the material between the grooves with a rabbet plane and – if you have one – a small hollow plane, such as a No. 6.

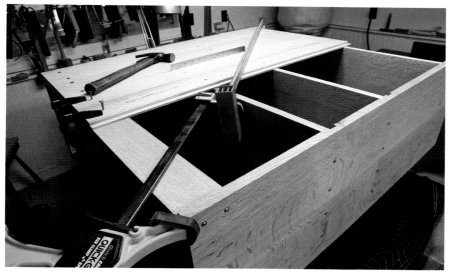

After plowing two grooves in the stiles, shape the interior bit into a curve with a rabbet plane. Then finish up with a small hollow plane.

Here I'm pulling the case square with two clamps. I then nail the backboards in place. When I release the clamps, the carcase will remain square.

The last bit of work on the face frame before the piercings is to saw out the feet. Cut them with a frame saw and clean up the cuts with rasps.

Gothic Tracery

The geometric pierced shapes in the stiles are easy to make, even if you've never carved before. You don't even need carving tools to do the job. Here are the tools I used:

- A ½" Forstner bit to poke holes in the waste.
- An electric jigsaw to remove most of the waste.
- A coarse cabinet rasp to shape the openings.
- ¼" and ½" chisels to bevel the edges and make the triangular chip carvings.
- A fine rasp to clean up the details.

You can create patterns for the piercings using a compass and straightedge or you can download the full-size patterns for free at popularwoodworking.com/feb15. Apply the pattern directly to the work using spray adhesive, then bore out most of the waste with a drill.

After sawing out the waste, clean up the openings with a cabinet rasp. I used a 10" rasp with hand-stitched teeth that were fairly coarse – a 9 grain. The goal is to make the walls square and the lines fluid.

With the openings shaped, bevel their interior edges with a ½" chisel, working bevel-down for the most part. The bevel

Apply the pattern with spray adhesive and drill out the waste with a ¹/₂" Forstner bit.

should be only about ¼" deep to create the three-dimensional effect. If you are using oak, you should sharpen the chisel frequently for the best results.

Then, clean up the cuts with a fine rasp, shaping the bars of the Gothic windows. I used a 7" modeler's rasp with 13-grain teeth. Follow up with sandpaper if you like.

Many of the corners of the tracery have triangular chip-carved details. These are easily made with bench chisels. Chop straight down on the three facets of the detail. Then pare out the waste toward the chops. Repeat these two operations until the detail is as deep as

Use a jigsaw set with minimal orbit to remove waste as close to the line as possible. I used a standard jigsaw blade for this. I tried using a narrow blade intended for scrollwork, but it deflected too much.

The triangular depressions at the corners of the piercings are easy to make with a chisel and mallet.

It's easier to rasp vertically if you hold the handle with one hand and the tip of the rasp with the other. Check your work with a square until you get a feel for the operation.

The pilot holes for the nails should be about two-thirds the length of the nail. That will give the nail the holding power it needs to keep the face frame on.

you want it – mine are ³⁄₁₆" deep.

With the piercings complete, glue the face frame together and attach it to the front of the carcase with 6d wrought nails. Because the wide stiles will expand and contract significantly, I would not glue the stiles to the sides of the carcase. The wood movement might crack the carcase.

If you do want to use glue, apply it to the shelves near the door opening only.

The Door

Most aumbries have a single door. There is evidence that this aumbry had two, and the lower one is missing. I like the open space below, so I made only one door that enclosed the top two shelves.

The door is just a slab of oak with two geometric piercings. Make the crease mouldings and piercings using the same techniques as on the face frame stiles. I used a blacksmith-made lock and H-hinges, which were installed with wrought nails.

Installing hardware with nails is a bit stressful at first because there are no do-overs. Once you clinch the nails, prying them out can damage the door or stile. So you need your door to fit right the first time and clench the nails

with confidence – loose nails are no good.

The finish is simply boiled linseed oil. Apply thin coats and allow each coat to dry thoroughly before adding another – about two hours is typical. After five or six coats, add a coat of beeswax and buff it out. That's one traditional finish for early pieces such as this.

If you want more protection, consider adding a little varnish and mineral spirits to the oil to make a wipe-on oil/varnish blend. It's not traditional, but it will offer more protection and look the part.

And speaking of looking the part, if you want to go 100-percent authentic, cover the interior piercings with some undyed linen that is secured with iron tacks.

Supplies

Peter Ross

peterrossblacksmith.com
or 919-663-3309

Blacksmith-made hinges, locks and nails

Tremont Nail

tremontnail.com
or 800-835-0121

Rosehead and other cut nails

Horton Brasses

horton-brasses.com or 800-754-9127

1 pair iron H-hinges, 4" (#HF-7)

Call for prices.

Furniture Fundamentals: Casework. Copyright © 2016 by Popular Woodworking. Printed and bound in China. All rights reserved. No part of this book may be reproduced in any form or by any electronic or mechanical means including information storage and retrieval systems without permission in writing from the publisher, except by a reviewer, who may quote brief passages in a review. Published by Popular Woodworking Books, an imprint of F+W Media, Inc., 10151 Carver Rd. Blue Ash, Ohio, 45236. (800) 289-0963. First edition.

Distributed in Canada by Fraser Direct
100 Armstrong Avenue
Georgetown, Ontario L7G 5S4
Canada

Distributed in the U.K. and Europe by
F+W Media International, LTD
Pynes Hill Court
Pynes Hill
Rydon Lane
Exeter
EX2 5SP
Tel: +44 1392 797680

Visit our website at popularwoodworking.com or our consumer website at shopwoodworking.com for more woodworking information projects.

Other fine Popular Woodworking Books are available from your local bookstore or direct from the publisher.

ISBN-13: 978-1-4403-4878-5

20   19   18   17   16   5   4   3   2   1

Editor: Scott Francis
Designers: Daniel T. Pessell, Angela Wilcox
Production coordinator: Debbie Thomas

About the Authors

CHUCK BENDER
Chuck is a former senior editor with *Popular Woodworking Magazine*; he has been a professional woodworker for several decades.

LONNIE BIRD
Lonnie is a master woodworking instructor and fine furniture craftsman. Learn more at lonniebird.com.

MEGAN FITZPATRICK
Megan is the editor of *Popular Woodworking Magazine*.

GLEN D. HUEY
Glen is a former senior editor with *Popular Woodworking Magazine* and the author of several woodworking books.

BILL HYLTON
Bill is the author of several books about furniture construction and router operations.

FRANK KLAUSZ
Frank is a master cabinetmaker, author and owner of Frank's Cabinet Shop in Pluckermin, N.J.

MARIO RODRIGUEZ
Mario has more than 30 years' experience as woodworker, teacher and writer. He now is co-owner of the Philadelphia Furniture Workshop.

CHRISTOPHER SCHWARZ
Chris is a former editor of *Popular Woodworking Magazine* (now contributing editor) and is the editor at Lost Art Press.

TROY SEXTON
Troy Sexton designs and builds custom furniture and is a private woodworking instructor in Sunbury, Ohio, for his company, Sexton Classic American Furniture.

STEVE SHANESY
Steve is a former editor and publisher of *Popular Woodworking Magazine* and Popular Woodworking Books.

JIM STACK
Jim is a former senior editor of *Popular Woodworking Books* and is the author of numerous woodworking books.

FRANK STRAZZA
Frank is an award-winning furniture maker and a woodworking instructor at the Heritage School of Woodworking in Waco, Texas.

DAVID THIEL
David is a former senior editor for *Popular Woodworking Magazine* and now works with videos under the *Popular Woodworking* brand.

MATTHEW TEAGUE
Matthew is a furniture maker and writer based in Nashville, Tenn. He is a former editor of *Popular Woodworking Magazine*.

ROY UNDERHILL
Roy is the host of the long-running PBS television series "The Woodwright's Shop."

Metric Conversion Chart

TO CONVERT	TO	MULTIPLY BY
Inches	Centimeters	2.54
Centimeters	Inches	0.4
Feet	Centimeters	30.5
Centimeters	Feet	0.03
Yards	Meters	0.9
Meters	Yards	1.1

a content + ecommerce company

Read This Important Safety Notice

To prevent accidents, keep safety in mind while you work. Use the safety guards installed on power equipment; they are for your protection.

When working on power equipment, keep fingers away from saw blades, wear safety goggles to prevent injuries from flying wood chips and sawdust, wear hearing protection and consider installing a dust vacuum to reduce the amount of airborne sawdust in your woodshop.

Don't wear loose clothing, such as neckties or shirts with loose sleeves, or jewelry, such as rings, necklaces or bracelets, when working on power equipment. Tie back long hair to prevent it from getting caught in your equipment.

People who are sensitive to certain chemicals should check the chemical content of any product before using it.

Due to the variability of local conditions, construction materials, skill levels, etc., neither the author nor Popular Woodworking Books assumes any responsibility for any accidents, injuries, damages or other losses incurred resulting from the material presented in this book.

The authors and editors who compiled this book have tried to make the contents as accurate and correct as possible. Plans, illustrations, photographs and text have been carefully checked. All instructions, plans and projects should be carefully read, studied and understood before beginning construction.

Prices listed for supplies and equipment were current at the time of publication and are subject to change.

Ideas • Instruction • Inspiration

Receive FREE downloadable bonus materials when you sign up for our FREE newsletter at **popularwoodworking.com**.

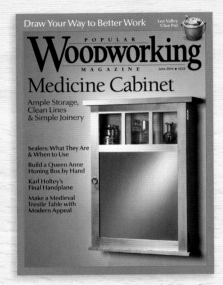

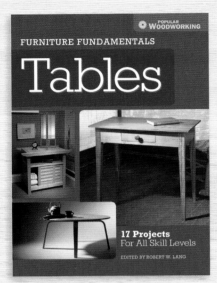

Find the latest issues of *Popular Woodworking Magazine* on newsstands, or visit **popularwoodworking.com**.

These and other great Popular Woodworking products are available at your local bookstore, woodworking store or online supplier. Visit our website at **shopwoodworking.com**.

Popular Woodworking Videos

Subscribe and get immediate access to the web's best woodworking subscription site. You'll find more than 400 hours of woodworking video tutorials and full-length video workshops from world-class instructors on workshops, projects, SketchUp, tools, techniques and more!

videos.popularwoodworking.com

Visit our Website

Find helpful and inspiring articles, videos, blogs, projects and plans at **popularwoodworking.com**.

 For behind the scenes information, become a fan at **Facebook.com/ popularwoodworking**.

 For more tips, clips and articles, follow us at **twitter.com/pweditors**.

 For visual inspiration, follow us at **pinterest.com/popwoodworking**.

 For free videos visit **youtube.com/popwoodworking**.